Shane O'Neill

Shane O'Neill

CIARAN BRADY

✦

Published on behalf of
the Historical Association of Ireland

UNIVERSITY COLLEGE DUBLIN PRESS
Preas Choláiste Ollscoile Bhaile Átha Cliath
2015

First published 1996 on behalf of the
Historical Association of Ireland by
Dundalgan Press, Dundalk

This New Edition first published 2015
in collaboration with the
Historical Association of Ireland by
University College Dublin Press

ISBN 978–1–910820–05–6
ISSN 2009–1397

University College Dublin Press
UCD Humanities Institute, Room H103, Belfield,
Dublin 4, Ireland
www.ucdpress.ie

Cataloguing in Publication data available from the British Library

Typeset in Scotland in Ehrhardt by Ryan Shiels
Text design by Lyn Davies
Printed in Dublin on acid-free paper by
SPRINT-print

CONTENTS

For Fiachra and Oisín

*

FOREWORD

Originally conceived over a decade ago to place the lives of leading figures in Irish history against the background of new research on the problems and conditions of their times and modern assessments of their historical significance, the Historical Association of Ireland Life and Times series enjoyed remarkable popularity and success. A second series has now been planned in association with UCD Press in a new format and with fuller scholarly apparatus. Encouraged by the reception given to the earlier series, the volumes in the new series will be expressly designed to be of particular help to students preparing for the Leaving Certificate, for GCE Advanced Level and for undergraduate history courses as well as appealing to the happily insatiable appetite for new views of Irish history among the general public.

CIARAN BRADY
Historical Association of Ireland

PREFACE

I have taken advantage of this second, enlarged edition of a study first published in 1996 to update and revise both the text and bibliography in order to take account of recent research and commentary. I have been concerned in particular to expand two themes. One has been the degree to which the posthumous myth of 'Shane the Proud's impossible personal character was a conscious fabrication of his contemporary enemies designed to obscure the profound ideological challenges which, largely inadvertently, he placed before them. A second related theme further developed here is the manner in which the particular challenges posed by Shane to uncritical governing assumptions concerning the natural superiority of the English legal and constitutional tradition fed into more immediate and more urgent concerns relating to the uncertain prospects of the early Elizabethan regime in regard to European dynastic politics in general, and Scottish politics in particular. In part accidental, and in some part quite deliberate, the tendency of the major figures of Elizabethan politics to immerse Shane's specific claims into the depths of these broader international contests was to render the possibility of arriving at a peaceful and stable settlement in Ulster immeasurably more difficult than it might otherwise have been.

In preparing this edition for publication I have been in receipt of the inestimable expertise of Noelle Moran and Damien Lynam at UCD Press. The National Library has once again been generous in regard to the cover illustration. But older debts accrued all those years ago are still pending. I want to thank Aoife Nic Réamoinn for her tolerance of a ghostly but extremely intrusive house-guest, the details of whose career seemed to acquire an increasingly acute relevance to the routines of our everyday life as time went on. My good friend Michael Quigley has been, as ever, an unfailing source of encouragement and consolation. Ken Nicholls, who knows far more about O'Neill and Ulster than I shall ever learn, has been unstinting in his provision of evidence and advice. Eugene Doyle, my fellow-editor, has been both an inspiration and an effective task-master. Colm Croker, a saint among copy-editors, was immensely generous with his time and expertise.

Finally, I should apologise to the spirit of Seán (*anglice* Shan) Ó Neill to whose first name the final *e* was never applied during his lifetime. I can only plead that this unscholarly surrender to later English convention has been made in an effort to make him appear less alien and less threatening to anglophone ears, and is a concession of which, as the evidence below indicates, he himself would have approved.

CIARAN BRADY
September 2015

CHRONOLOGY OF O'NEILL'S LIFE
AND TIMES

1519
Conn Bacach O'Neill becomes the O'Neill.

1528/30?
Birth of Shane O'Neill.

1534–6
Kildare rebellion deprives O'Neill of his principal ally.

1541
June Act for the kingly title; initiation of the policy of surrender and regrant.
December O'Neill submits to St Leger.

1542
Conn Bacach O'Neill created earl of Tyrone.
His son Feardorcha (*alias* Mathew) created baron of Dungannon.

1548
Shane's first recorded action in raid on Clandeboy.
Nicholas Bagenal established in Newry.

1549
Shane participates in O'Neill raid on Maguire.

1551

Civil war in Tír Eoghain.

Conn Bacach is arrested.

Dungannon narrowly misses killing Shane in chance encounter.

1552

Shane triumphs in O'Neill civil war.

1553

St Leger returns to Ireland.

Shane becomes pensioner of the crown.

1554

Kildare campaigns with Shane in Ulster.

1555

Hugh MacNeill Óg O'Neill of Clandeboy killed.

1556

May St Leger recalled; Thomas Radcliffe, earl of Sussex, becomes lord
   deputy.

1557

October Sussex campaigning in Ulster, burns Armagh.

1558

Feardorcha (*alias* Mathew), 1st baron of Dungannon murdered.

1559

July Conn Bacach dies; Shane proclaimed O'Neill at Tullaghogue,
   petitions to be recognised as earl of Tyrone.

1560

May Sussex secures Elizabeth's agreement for war against Shane.

August coalition against Shane dissolves.

1561

May Shane seizes Calvagh O'Donnell and his wife.

June Shane declared a traitor by printed proclamation.

July Sussex's campaign army routed by Shane.

1562

January Shane submits before Queen Elizabeth, commences negotiations at court.

April Brian, 2nd baron of Dungannon, murdered.

May Shane departs from court.

September–November Shane campaigns in south Ulster – repeated raids on the Pale.

1563

March–April Sussex's campaign against Shane collapses.

11 September Treaty of Drumcree.

November further negotiations elaborating the terms of Drumcree.

1564

May–June Shane invades Tír Conaill and devastates the country.

September Shane's unsuccessful assault on MacDonnells.

October Shane revisits Tír Conaill, establishing garrisons.

1565

May Shane defeats MacDonnells at Glentaisie (formerly misidentified as the adjacent Glenshesk)

October Shane invades Connacht.

1566

January Lord Deputy Sir Henry Sidney arrives in Ireland.

May Sir Francis Knollys arrives on commission.

April–June Shane negotiates with Charles IX of France and the earl of Argyll.

August Shane evacuates Armagh.

September–November Sidney campaigns in Ulster.

26 October Calvagh O'Donnell dies – Hugh claims succession.

November Shane attacks Derry – Randolph killed.

1567

21 April explosion destroys English garrison at Derry.

8 May Shane defeated by the O'Donnells and the MacSwineys at Farsetmore.

2 June Shane killed by the MacDonnells at Cushendun.

1569

11 March Act of attainder declaring Shane a traitor passed in the Irish parliament – its preamble offers first official history of his life and times.

CHAPTER I

The Legend of Shane the Proud: A Myth and Its Uses

If there is one thing that most people remember about Shane O'Neill, it is that he was proud. Although most of the details of his life have long been forgotten, or confused with those of his greater namesake (and bitter enemy) Hugh, the legend of Shane the Proud – of the brave warrior brought down by his own wilful and over-reaching ambition – has exerted a hold over the popular imagination for centuries, sustained by successive commentators, sympathetic and hostile alike.

The durability of this summary character description is, on the face of it, odd. For the fact is that we know very little about Shane as an individual, and what little has been said about him has been speculative and highly suspect. We do not know what he looked like (the cover illustration is a piece of nostalgic romantic invention), whether he was tall or short, clean shaven or bearded, dark or fair. The very year of his birth is uncertain, and the circumstances of his death are shrouded in doubt.

His detractors, though, from Campion and Hooker in the sixteenth century to Froude and Bagwell in the nineteenth, have been eager to fill out this shadowy physical form with other grave defects of character to complement his cardinal sin of pride.[1] That Shane was a 'sot', a drunk who ensured that his wine cellar was constantly stocked with 200 tuns of wine, and who devised a cure for hangover (which involved having himself buried up to his neck in hot ash), was a frequently attested though largely uncorroborated fact.

> Yet was he never satisfied until he had swallowed up vast quantities of usquebagh or aqua vite of that Country wherof so unmeasurably would he drink and boose.[2]

This was John Hooker, writing twenty years after Shane's death; and though the story came late, and from a distinctly hostile source, it soon became orthodox.

That he was also sexually depraved is another alleged truth advanced, though with rather more delicacy, by his critics. Rumours that he had revived certain bestial practices anciently associated with the inauguration of Gaelic chieftains were knowingly referred to. His complicated marital arrangements were deplored. And lurid reports of Shane's treatment of Calvagh O'Donnell and his wife, to the effect that he had kept O'Donnell chained and on all fours in a cage in his bedchamber while he repeatedly ravished his unhappy spouse, were offered as proof of Shane's total degeneracy.

There was more. His gluttony, well attested by Campion and Hooker, was repeatedly reaffirmed. His cowardice was declared self-evident in his unwillingness to confront an English army in open battle, and in his propensity to vanish when such an army approached. And his cruelty was confirmed by stories of his sadistic delight in torturing victims to death, and (more bathetically) in his casual murder of an unfortunate he came upon enjoying an English biscuit.[3]

All of these features of Shane's perversity – his drunkenness, his violence and, above all, his pride – were appropriately reconfigured in the officially recorded account of his death at the hands of the Scots in 1567. While negotiating with his erstwhile friends and recent enemies, Shane – so the story goes – was at a banquet feasting and drinking. After a while, as might be expected from such men, the talk turned to sex. Fired by drink, Shane's secretary boasted that his master was a match for any Scotswoman, even the Queen of Scots herself. The Scots took offence, and when Shane intervened to affirm the truth of his prowess, they fell on him and cut him to pieces. Thus perished Shane, just as he had lived, in a welter of violence, drunkenness and pride.[4]

The response of Irish nationalist historians to this hostile and predominantly English portrait of a wild and wicked man brought down by his own vices has been curiously ambiguous.[5] Many, like John Mitchel, Thomas O'Gorman and the anonymous authors of two short lives: *The Story of Shane O'Neill*, and *Seághan an Díomais*, pointed to the extremely biased sources from which such stories emerged as a means of questioning their veracity.[6] But having done so, most simply went on to rehearse or acknowledge these well-worn traditions. In regard to Shane's supposed boozing, no one, for instance, seemed to consider that the wine stocks at Dundrum served as part of an important element in Shane's financial and commercial relations with the Western Isles, or pointed out that contemporaries never remarked on the gargantuan scale of his habit in the manner they were shortly to report on the feats of his immediate successor, Turlough Luineach; and though his resort to ash-pit, if true, may have been as innocent as an effort to find relief from arthritis (it was a commonly used folk medicine) Hooker's inference that Shane was dissolute rather than decrepit was rarely challenged.[7]

No one remarked that the story of his conduct toward O'Donnell was based entirely on the *ex parte* statements of Calvagh himself, or that O'Donnell's wife, Catherine MacLean, was suspected by contemporaries of having colluded in the kidnapping, and that having refused to return to her husband when the opportunity arose, she elected to stay with Shane until the end.[8] Instead, almost all of Shane's sympathisers regretfully admitted his fault in this matter, some adding the caveat that little more could have been expected from men of his time.[9] But even among the few stalwarts, like John Mitchel, who refused to have any truck with such scandals, the violent manner of Shane's death was accepted as inevitable on the grounds that, for all his abilities, the essential and ultimately fatal element in his character was, as Mitchel put it, 'his indomitable pride'.[10]

The nature of this defining sobriquet, 'Shane the Proud', employed both by friends and enemies alike, is not without interest. It has roots, no doubt, in the harping of Campion and Hooker on Shane's habitual insolence and arrogance. But the stigmatic title appears also to have had a specifically Irish origin in the Gaelic *Seán an Díomais*, which, according to John O'Donovan and other authorities, had made its appearance by the end of the sixteenth century, and was soon to be translated into the early texts of Irish nationalism as 'Johannes Superbus'.[11] The Gaelic title and its Latin derivative are especially significant, for here the pejorative connotations of pride, left somewhat muted in English are quite unmistakable. *Díomas*, rather than *bród* or *uaimhreacht* translates unambiguously as arrogance, scorn, contempt, vainglory, making O'Neill's title more accurately rendered into English not as Shane the Proud but simply as Vain Shane.

The ready adoption by Shane's natural sympathisers of his enemies' account of his ruin and the fatal flaw which had impelled him toward it is, at first sight, peculiar. But it becomes less so once it is related to the story of that other proud man of sixteenth-century Ireland whose vanity has traditionally been held responsible for similarly fatal consequences – Thomas, Lord Offaly, or 'Silken Thomas'. The legend of the narcissistic young lord who precipitated the Kildare rebellion with all its terrible consequences for the Geraldines by his intemperate response to deliberate provocation had its origins, significantly perhaps, in the very place where Campion first floated the myth of Shane O'Neill, the home of Richard Stanihurst in Dublin. The motive behind Stanihurst's original account of Silken Thomas's revolt has now been made abundantly clear. Through it the historian aimed to exceptionalise the disaster of 1534, to evade the complicated forces which actually brought it about, and so to minimise its significance to later generations.[12] The circumstantial differences between the Anglo-Irish lord and the Ulster chief, and the ideological intent of those who sought to 'interpret' them, are obvious. Yet the attribution of the same moral defect has in both cases served a similar explanatory purpose. What, for all their differences, Offaly and O'Neill had in common is that both, driven by personal impulses, wilfully mis-perceived their true historical role, and in doing so inadvertently triggered events which were to be fateful for the subsequent development of Irish history. Shane's desire to be accepted by the English as earl of Tyrone, his opportunist and unprincipled dealings with the Scots, and, above all, his ruthless oppression of his Gaelic Irish neighbours in Ulster made it extremely difficult – even for the most sympathetic writers – to accommodate him within the nationalist historical canon.[13] And, in the end, moreover, he lost, not in some grand patriotic struggle, but in what was first reported as a shabby intrigue, thereby laying the whole of Ulster open to irreversible English penetration. Supplied thus with the evidence both of his political and moral ambivalence, and also with the brute fact of his failure, the temptation to explain Shane away through wild idiosyncrasy became overwhelming, through a regretful acceptance of his enemies' unsubstantiated claims that the man was both personally and historically impossible.

What has been on display here from both sides is, of course, the dominance of ideological preference over historical imagination. In explaining Shane by reference to undemonstrable and quite circular psychological characteristics, his historians – nationalist and imperialist alike – have been enabled at once to reaffirm conventional interpretative prejudices and also to evade the burden of undertaking an examination of the complicated circumstances and contingent forces which enframed his public life.

Yet within this silent conspiracy of opponents, there is an even richer irony at play whose meaning and implication has been all too neglected. For the posthumous character assassination of the assassinated Shane was no accident. Nor can it be accounted for simply by reference to the crude ethnological stereotypes which have so often been invoked to explain English attitudes toward Ireland in the sixteenth century. It was, instead, an integral part of a deliberate strategy of historical revision which found its earliest expression some two years after Shane's death as part of the extraordinary and lengthy preamble which preceded the statute attainting Shane as a traitor in 1569. But, more interestingly, the hidden roots of this subtle propaganda campaign can be traced a further seven years back to the time of Shane's celebrated visit to the court of Elizabeth I in 1562.[14]

In the course of those negotiations – the context and course of which are considered in detail in chapter 4 below – Shane argued that the treaty of 1542 between the crown and his father Conn Bacach which issued in the formal surrender of the O'Neill lordship and its transformation into the earldom of Tyrone contained elements whose legal significance had not been fully appreciated. Amidst the many rights formally surrendered by Conn Bacach and returned to him as earl of Tyrone were some which were not attached to his person as an individual but were derived from prior obligations which he had assumed as the 'officer' of his people, the O'Neill. It was not part of Shane's intention to claim these rights for himself in perpetuity; in fact he was willing to put such matters on the table for detailed bargaining later on. But his major point, more specific, more immediately pertinent, and yet more subtle, was that, since the initial negotiations about the establishment of the earldom of Tyrone which had begun with the then O'Neill were clearly imperfect, based on this confusion, it was necessary that they be recommenced. And granted this false start, it was clear that the only individual with whom the process could be recommenced was Shane himself, for two distinct reasons: first because he was the undisputed O'Neill, the figure toward whom the original address had been made; and secondly because he was, as of 1562, the only legitimate heir of Conn Bacach who had signed the original indentures.[15]

This was an exquisitely clever argument. And had the circumstances surrounding the case been different to what they actually were in 1562, it might even have been effective. But the implications of Shane's specific claim were of far wider significance than the dispute about the earldom of Tyrone. If Shane's arguments were acknowledged, did they not suggest that all of the several earlier negotiations which the agents of the crown had conducted with other major dynasties across the island were subject equally to such a challenge? And, if this were the case, with whom, if anyone at all, was the crown to negotiate?

Solutions to this embarrassment were not impossible: Shane himself suggested several. But once, and for the complex and sorry reasons to be detailed below, they failed in the case of Shane O'Neill, broader explanations of that failure needed to be found. Thus there emerged the great and radical revision of Irish history which appeared first, and not by coincidence, in the act attainting the traitorous subject Shane O'Neill. That new history, based both on authorities such as Geoffrey of Monmouth and Gildas (already regarded with great dubiety in advanced Elizabethan scholarly circles) and on unverifiable anecdote, was designed with a specific purpose: the need to address the challenge posed by the argument

raised by Shane O'Neill.[16] Resting on such authorities, the new
history claimed that all of the inhabitants of Ireland had been made
subject to the crown of England because the great (and legendary)
King Gurmundus, son of the king of Britain and lord of the
territory of Bayon in northern Spain, had bestowed on the very
first Irishmen Hiberus and Hermon the right to settle in Ireland.
The historical veracity of this tale was of secondary importance to
its contemporary relevance. For its truth, confirmed by statutory
authority, entailed that all of the inhabitants of the island of
Ireland were, from the beginning, the subjects of the sovereigns
of Britain.

    An outrageous imperialism, as it may seem, the intent of this
assertion was not, however, broadly or crudely assertive. It was,
rather, narrowly conceived, and strategically directed. Since all of
the inhabitants of Ireland, it affirmed, were equally subjects of the
kings of Britain, the claims of an intermediate level of 'captains',
chieftains or 'O's' or 'Mac's', or however they chose to describe
themselves, were simply usurpations perpetrated by individuals or
families without any constitutional or historical legitimacy. In
principle this would have allowed the crown simply to dismiss such
violators of the true relationship between the sovereign and its
true subjects. But in practice, given the passage of time, engage-
ment with such usurpers was preferable, as long as they were
willing to recognise their anomalous position, and to surrender it.
And this, according to the official view, was what had actually been
attempted in the several negotiations undertaken by the agents of
the Tudor crown. Many of these negotiations had been entirely
successful. But in certain instances, where the pleasures of untram-
melled power, and luxury, and tyranny had become so inordinate,
no accommodation was possible. Such was the case with the most
tyrannical war-lord of them all, Shane, whose violence, whose

drunkenness, whose sexual depravity and, above all, whose Luciferian pride, were emblems of his complete degeneracy.[17]

Ironically, this mode of historical re-interpretation precluded any brisk dismissal of Shane as an outlaw, in the manner in which countless other Irish war-lords had been disposed of in the past. Because of its insistence that Shane, like everyone else in Ireland from time immemorial, was a subject of the crown, it was requisite that he be treated as such and thus subjected to a formal attainder – a statutory declaration that, as all his vices proclaimed, he had indeed been corrupted in blood. Thus it was necessary also to acknowledge what Shane had always claimed, and what the crown had hitherto regarded as irrelevant to the treaty with Conn Bacach, that he was indeed the legitimate heir of his father – a recognition belatedly granted not as a grudging concession, but as a means of sealing his extinction.

Thus the mythologising of 'Shane the Proud' was not simply the natural by-product of English cultural prejudice; but a stratagem conceived to meet precise and acute political imperatives. The propaganda campaign initiated in the preamble to the act attainting Shane and developed by Campion was further elaborated by John Hooker in his contribution on recent Irish history to Holinshed's *Chronicles*, and reaffirmed in Camden's account of Shane's mission to court.[18] It was sustained perhaps to even greater effect in writings produced for circulation among the policy-making elite such as Lord Burghley's 'Memorandum for Ulster' or Sir Henry Sidney's 'Memoir of service'; or in supplementary materials such as the genealogies drawn up (in English) for dispatch to Whitehall purporting to show that Shane was the only legitimate son of Conn Bacach.[19] And it received its most ironic representation in the extended use made of it by Hugh O'Neill in his petitions to have the rights granted to him as earl of Tyrone seriously extended.[20]

It is this murky and deeply deceptive background to all the supposed degenerate qualities attached to Shane that makes it all the more urgent that we abandon the deliberately misleading and ultimately futile speculations about Shane's personality, and address instead a number of demonstrable facts concerning his external circumstances whose manifold implications – lost amidst all the talk about his character – have yet to be explored. We know, for instance, that in becoming the O'Neill Shane inherited a complex set of problems and responsibilities that was a collective bequest from his predecessors who had occupied this pivotal role in Ulster. We know also that when he assumed what he fatefully described as the 'office' of O'Neillship, the traditional difficulties of his place had been made even more dangerous by the operation of a number of forces over which he himself had no control: the accelerating instability of several neighbouring lordships, the increasing influence of independent Scottish forces in the province, and the gradual reassertion of a direct interest in Ulster by the Tudor crown. And finally we can say that, through an accident of birth, Shane succeeded to all of this dubious dynastic inheritance under the most contested of circumstances.

None of these questions can claim to lead to some alternative judgement of the character of Shane O'Neill: but they do allow an inquiry more fruitful than any of the uncritically confident verdicts with which he has been disposed of in the past. Although it is fatuous to speculate as to whether Shane was a vicious, degenerate, or even a particularly vain man, it is at least useful to consider what was really at stake when he inherited the O'Neill lordship and all its problems early in 1559.

CHAPTER 2

The Problems of O'Neill Lordship, 1241–1541

GEOGRAPHY

The fundamental problem of the O'Neill lordship can be expressed in simple geographical terms. It was awkwardly shaped, poorly defined, and badly fractured from within: it was, for the purposes of political coherence, too big. The ancient kingdom of Cinéal Eoghain over which the O'Neills had claimed sovereignty since the late twelfth century was a large sprawling territory, spreading northward and westward from the centre of Ulster to the very tip of the Inishowen peninsula and southward through Armagh, bordering on the drumlin country of Cavan and Monaghan, and stretching even to the borders of the Pale shire of County Louth. By the beginning of the sixteenth century the O'Neills had lost practical control over Inishowen to the O'Dohertys (though they never surrendered the claim): yet their lordship of Tír Eoghain still encompassed all the modern counties of Tyrone, Derry and Armagh, with significant, though disputed, territories in Antrim and Down.[1]

Yet it was neither a stable nor a well-integrated entity. Both to the west and to the east its borders were uncertain, while its natural boundaries formed by the rivers Foyle and Bann offered no permanent stability, for each was easily fordable at several places and offered little obstacle to raiding parties or invading armies. To the south the lordship was less obviously permeable, though the gradually dispersed nature of the drumlin country none-the-less rendered its southern inhabitants vulnerable to raids and ambushes at innumerable places. But the most serious geographical problem that confronted the O'Neills came from within. For the lordship was sharply divided by the Sperrins, a formidable range of mountains which, running from the south-west to north-east, effectively sliced the territory in half. Thus with weak or indefinite borders on most sides and with the Sperrins serving as a powerful barrier in the centre, Tír Eoghain had tended to divide into two distinct political zones around two great loci of military and political power, Strabane in the north-west and Dungannon in the south-east.[2]

The daunting strategic problems to which these geographical conditions gave rise were balanced, however, by the considerable political and economic opportunities which they also made available. The lordship rested on some of the richest soils in the province which supported a mixed and relatively buoyant agricultural economy that in peacetime was capable of sustaining large herds of cattle and an awesome number of unproductive fighting men. The north-western region of Tír Eoghain was the most fertile and richest portion of the lordship, but it was also the most vulnerable to incursion from the O'Donnells and their supporters in neighbouring Tír Conaill, and the most in need, therefore, of military protection. The south-eastern portion of the lordship was somewhat less economically blessed, but it was also less politically challenged. For there the surrounding lordships of O'Reilly, Mac Mahon, O'Hanlon and Magennis and the Anglo-Irish settlements east of the Bann were smaller, weaker and quite disunited. And so the fordable rivers and negotiable passes which in other circumstances might have posed a threat offered instead an opportunity to the O'Neills of establishing a loose suzerainty over their weaker neighbours, by diplomacy, intrigue, intimidation and overt aggression.

Thus between Tír Eoghain's rich but vulnerable sector and its less fertile but strategically advantaged zone a kind of symbiotic relationship began to evolve by which the militarily stronger part imposed a form of protection upon its neighbour and exacted in return the resources which sustained its own costly regime. In this relationship it was the priorities of the military men which necessarily prevailed. For the maintenance of the internal integrity of Tír Eoghain was essential to the preservation of their own form of rule. Thus the chronic aggression of the O'Neill overlords, their suppression of dissent from within and their determination to crush any challenge from outside with a ruthlessness which was a hallmark of their dealings with all of their neighbours, represented no simple-minded belligerence but an acceptance of the conditions laid down by geography: a recognition of the reality that if they were to survive, the O'Neills must also dominate.

HISTORY

The political history of the O'Neills in the later middle ages may be understood as the product of this restless and urgent imperative. From their emergence as a political force in the late twelfth century the O'Neills were aggressive and expansionist, and increasingly that expansionism was orchestrated from the south from their great fortress of Dungannon, rather than from Strabane. Though it had been threatened for almost a century before, O'Neill dominance in Tír Eoghain was finally secured at the battle of Caiméirge in 1241 when the power of their rivals, the MacLoughlins, was finally extinguished. The destruction of the MacLoughlins, whose power had been centred on the north-western sector, marked the triumph of the poorer, more aggressive southern half, the eclipse of Strabane and the elevation of Dungannon.[3]

But having displaced the MacLoughlins, the O'Neills now inherited, though in reverse, the same deeply fissured lordship, which their predecessors had found so difficult to control. Their attempts to meet the challenge were at once natural and fraught with danger. In the late twelfth and early thirteenth centuries the O'Neill lords sought to maintain control over the north-western sector by delegating military responsibility for the area to one of their elder sons, usually to the one considered most likely to succeed as the next chieftain. This was what was attempted by the first great O'Neill leader, Brian of the battle of Down (O'Neill, 1238–60) with his son Niall, by Domhnall O'Neill (O'Neill, *c.*1283–1325) with his son Seán, by Aodh Reamhar (O'Neill, 1345–64) with his son Domhnall, and by Niall Mór (O'Neill, 1364–97) with his son Énrí Aimhréidh, and so on with every successive O'Neill throughout the fifteenth century.[4] But from the outset such a holding operation entailed serious risks, as the immediate descendants of these delegated officers began to declare their independence of, or opposition to, the one who actually succeeded as O'Neill. Thus Niall mac Brian became an implacable opponent of Domhnall O'Neill as chieftain, forcing him to recognise for a time an actual division of the lordship; while Domhnall, the son of Aodh Reamhar, refused to acknowledge the chieftainship of his brother Niall Mór until the close of the 1370s. In the early fifteenth century the sons of Énrí Aimhréidh (Sliocht Énrí) plunged the lordship into a civil war that ended only with the death of their leader in battle and the triumph of Niall Mór's grandson, Eoghan, in 1432.[5] This Eoghan, the first to be styled 'the Great O'Neill', established an unprecedented authority in Tír Eoghain until his peaceful resignation of office in favour of his son Énrí in 1455. But once again he had fomented a major challenge to his successor many years previously by delegating the north-west to another son, Art, whose sons, in alliance with Sliocht Énrí Aimhréidh, mounted an increasingly effective campaign against Énrí that finally broke his power altogether in the early 1480s.[6]

In destroying the authority of Énrí (O'Neill, 1455–83), these groups were greatly sustained by the support and actual intervention of the very dynasty against whom they had been commissioned to defend the north-west in the first place, O'Donnells of Tír Conaill, who had been exploiting internal tensions within Tír Eoghain with greater or lesser success for centuries.[7] This long war with the O'Donnells which preoccupied the O'Neills almost continually throughout their ascendancy can generally be accounted as a stalemate. A brief review of the annals may give the impression that the O'Neills were more consistently successful in their forays than the O'Donnells, and it is true that the war contributed substantially to the failure of the O'Donnells to establish dynastic stability in Tír Conaill until the later fifteenth century. But there were real limitations to the O'Neills' achievement. They never succeeded in destroying the O'Donnells' power in Tír Conaill (as they had done with the MacLoughlins) or even in seriously damaging their provincial ambitions, especially toward the south and west. They never recovered Inishowen or the disputed borderland of Cinéal Moen, while the repeated efforts of successive O'Neill chieftains from Brian O'Neill in 1260 to Conn Bacach in the 1520s to organise a grand coalition in Ulster against the O'Donnells usually failed. Moreover, in the second half of the fifteenth century, the development which the O'Neills most feared began to take shape, with the consolidation of O'Donnell power in Tír Conaill under their immensely successful chieftain, Aodh Ruadh. Under Aodh Ruadh, O'Donnell intrigues became increasingly successful, until in 1498 he enjoyed the unprecedented and consummate achievement of imposing his own nominee, Domhnall, as the O'Neill.[8]

The O'Donnells thus greatly exacerbated the centrifugal tendencies of the north-west. But east of the Bann, and due in no small measure to the ruling families' preoccupation with the O'Donnells, even more decisive separatist tendencies began to emerge by the close of the fourteenth century within a colony established by the O'Neills themselves in the territory named, after the group who originally founded it, Clandeboy (Clann Aodha Buidhe).[9] Following the gradual collapse of the Anglo-Norman earldom of Ulster toward the middle of the fourteenth century, the O'Neills began a steady infiltration into east Ulster, first by means of diplomacy and intrigue, but increasingly after 1350 by armed intervention. Having established themselves as overlords in the territories of the old earldom, however, the Clandeboy O'Neills then declared themselves independent of the central dynasty and defied all of Tír Eoghain's attempts to exact tribute from them. In doing so they found natural allies among all the enemies of O'Neill in the province, especially the O'Donnells, and together these two lordships, though far separated from each other physically, fashioned a close alliance, often cemented by marriage and fosterage, against the great lordship which lay between them. Thus within little more than a century of the establishment of their hegemony in Tír Eoghain, the O'Neills found themselves surrounded by two lesser but powerful families, determined to resist all their expansionist ambitions.[10]

From about the late fourteenth century also, and with increasing importance thereafter, such resistance to the O'Neill was greatly strengthened through the employment by O'Donnell and the Clandeboy O'Neills of Scottish mercenary soldiers.[11] At first such forces were hired for short-term ends through temporary deals with the MacDonnell lords of the Isles. But over time the Scots began to establish a more permanent presence in Ulster politics as small settlements in Tír Conaill and a more significant bridgehead in the Glens of Antrim served as bases for more regular and more independent Scottish interventions. Scottish settlements in east Ulster did not seriously expand until the second quarter of the sixteenth century, but their proficiency in making available large numbers of trained troops at very short notice not only contributed greatly to the general militarisation of Ulster; it profoundly shaped the foreign and domestic policies of the great lordships as they sought to billet their increasingly large standing armies on their subjects and on their weaker neighbours.[12]

Such conditions applied most intensely in Tír Eoghain, where, challenged by Scots-importing enemies on both sides, the ruling dynasty was compelled to exact ever-increasing taxes on its own subjects and on its vassal lordships. The sixteenth-century version of the *Ceart Uí Néil*, a document which details the tributes demanded by O'Neill throughout the province was doubtless exaggerated.[13] But the extent and depth of its claims are evidence of how oppressive the O'Neills' ambitions actually were, while the manner in which the original text had been added to over the previous three centuries offered a clear indication that even now such demands had not reached their limit. As such, it was emblematic of the paradox that lay at the heart of O'Neill lordship: driven to pursue a persistently aggressive policy toward their neighbours in order to defend the ever-threatened internal coherence of their own lordship, the O'Neills inevitably provoked a universally hostile reaction which fuelled such internal fissures, causing them in turn to redouble their claims to provincial dominance and to extend their territorial and fiscal demands throughout the province. In seeking to maintain their own stability, the O'Neills had condemned themselves to a history of ceaseless war.

DIPLOMACY

Left as it stands, however, such an analysis would be somewhat simplistic. It would be wrong to assume that this complex of problems which faced the O'Neills rendered them uniquely vulnerable. For the same challenges of internal divisions and dynastic strife afflicted each of their major rivals in Ulster. In Tír Conaill the O'Donnells were almost constantly plagued by dynastic and territorial conflict. Even the great Aodh Ruadh faced bitter opposition when he sought to nominate his successor, and he never succeeded in subordinating the troublesome MacSwineys and O'Dohertys in his lordship.[14] In Clandeboy dynastic war was endemic, and the use by contenders of large numbers of Scots mercenaries frequently had the effect of reducing the lordship to chaos. It always remained possible for O'Neill, therefore, to exploit the systematic and periodic weaknesses of his enemies in a manner that ensured that whatever defeats and reversals they afflicted on him, no loss would ever prove decisive or irrecoverable.[15]

Yet though the O'Neills had never been singularly disadvantaged in the game of Ulster's politics, its mounting expense, its inherent unpredictability and of course its great personal dangers made such a game increasingly unattractive. Thus being neither blind to the paradoxical position in which geography and history had placed them, nor fatalistically committed to continuing on with the struggle until the bitter end, successive O'Neills sought to find some strategy alternative to permanent war which would enable them to stabilise their position in Ulster while preserving the exceptional authority to which they laid claim. And in pursuing this diplomatic alternative they looked beyond Ulster to the only comparable and sometimes superior power in Ireland, the English lordship.

Tír Eoghain's relationship with the English in Ireland in the later middle ages was a matter of some complexity which operated, often simultaneously, on four levels. At the simplest and most continuous level there were the O'Neills' regular dealings with the borderers of Meath and Louth, which for the most part resembled Tír Eoghain's relations with the lesser Ulster lordships in repeated patterns of feuding and alliance-making.[16] But beyond this the O'Neills' attitude toward the English lordship was somewhat complicated by the generally shadowy but sometimes real English provincial dominion, the earldom of Ulster.[17] Established in the late twelfth century, the earldom, which laid nominal claims to the whole province but which never actually extended west of the Bann, was in eclipse at the time of the rise of the O'Neills. But it was occasionally revived thereafter, first by Richard de Burgh close to the beginning of the fourteenth century and later by Roger Mortimer at its close.[18] The implications for the O'Neills of such intermittent reappearances were ambivalent. The obvious military challenge posed to their own authority in Ulster could not be ignored. Yet the broad provincial claims of the earls, which could never be enforced except through the consent of the native inhabitants, provided an indirect opportunity to the O'Neills of establishing their own provincial position by means of a treaty by which O'Neill would recognise the earl as his liege lord, and the earl would recognise O'Neill as his steward responsible for maintaining the obedience and peace of all the other Gaelic lords in Ulster. There is evidence that this is what the O'Neill chieftains attempted to negotiate with the de Burghs in the early fourteenth century. But the O'Neills' difficulty lay in the fact that, having aggressively reasserted their claims, the earls were unable to sustain a sufficient interest in Ulster to allow their would-be Irish allies a chance to play that role. In practice, then, the earldom remained a nuisance, incapable of establishing the provincial order for which the O'Neills had offered submission, but presenting by its theoretical existence a barrier to all of the O'Neills' efforts to find an alternative framework of stability in Ulster.[19]

There beckoned, however, one radical means of discounting the earldom altogether by exploiting a further, indeed the highest, level of relations between the O'Neills and the English: that was a direct relationship with the English crown itself.[20] A strategy first developed by Niall Mór O'Neill in his negotiations with Richard II in 1395 during which Richard came very close to recognising O'Neill as his direct vassal until, very late in the proceedings, he realised the constitutional implications of this effective suppression of the earldom of Ulster, and backed away.[21] But it reappeared in more viable circumstances when Edward of York, on whom the earldom had devolved, became the king of England in 1461.

As earl of Ulster, Edward's father, Richard, duke of York, had already visited Ireland in 1449, and concluded then an agreement with Eoghan O'Neill, confirming the old O'Neill ambition by recognising him as the earl's *mesne* lord in Ulster. The agreement might have had no more value than earlier efforts in this direction, except for the fact that when Edward became king, O'Neill's long-sought desire to be chief lord in Ulster under the crown appeared to have been attained. Throughout Edward's reign relations between the crown and O'Neill were unprecedentedly amicable. Not a single raid on the Pale was recorded, and O'Neill seems to have sought to defend the remnants of the old earldom in the east by making fairly constant war against the territory's principal enemies, the O'Neills of Clandeboy. It was at this time that the O'Neill came to be referred to in the official records in unparalleled terms of warmth as the king's good subject, servant, and even 'the king's friend'.[22]

Yet the difficulties which had undermined all previous efforts in relation to the earls of Ulster continued to plague this apparently stronger rapprochement. Although O'Neill succeeded in preventing his subjects from raiding the Pale or damaging the crown's other Irish allies, he could not, on his own, silence the Clandeboy O'Neills and the crown's other enemies in Ulster. These limits to his own power were reinforced by the weakness of his new royal ally, who proved unable to provide the military or diplomatic support which might have enabled O'Neill to fulfil their shared objectives in Ulster. After the debâcle of Sir John Tiptoft's governorship (1467–70), which alienated almost every major force in Ireland and seriously embarrassed O'Neill with his Irish and Anglo-Irish allies, Edward lost interest in Ireland, and when his successor Richard III became embroiled in a fatal civil war this experiment of dealing directly with the Yorkist kings ceased altogether.[23]

But the Yorkists' abandonment of their Ulster allies, in tandem with their gradual surrender of the whole of the Irish lordship to local interests, allowed for the development of a fourth level of relations between the O'Neills and the English colonists which had hitherto been the least promising of all. Traditionally, the attitude of the king's lieutenant toward Tír Eoghain had been defensive or, when the opportunity arose, frankly exploitative: the governors interfered in the north generally to mount punitive raids, to defend allies or, occasionally, to intervene in succession disputes. But in the early fourteenth century, during the eclipse of the earldom of Ulster and the development of separatist tendencies among the Anglo-Irish throughout the island, holders of the office began to develop a more sustained interest in Ulster politics with the view to encouraging stronger diplomatic and factional links with the Gaelic dynasties. The first great exponent of this strategy was James Butler, the 'White Earl' of Ormond (1405–52), who sought to establish a dynastic alliance with Eoghan O'Neill by marrying his niece Gormlaith to the O'Neill's son Énrí, and who demonstrated a

willingness both to ignore the Ulster earldom and recognise
O'Neill as the chief subject in the province. At first this new
alliance was extremely effective, and O'Neill served Ormond well
in offering protection to the Pale. But it weakened over time, and
by the close of Ormond's governorship, with the prospects of a
more attractive deal with the house of York enticing O'Neill, the
two were again at loggerheads. With the collapse of the Yorkist
alliance, however, O'Neill was once again compelled to seek accommodation with the absentee king's quasi-autonomous representative
in Ireland. This time he looked not to Ormond, but to the Butlers'
traditional rivals, the Fitzgeralds of Kildare.[24]

Some overtures toward the Geraldines on the part of O'Neill
have been discovered by historians as early as the late 1450s. But it
was not until the late 1470s that a firm alliance was concluded by
means of a marriage between Énrí O'Neill's son, Conn, and the
eighth earl of Kildare's sister Eleanor whose significance was
solemnly recognised by the Irish parliament in a declaration that
Conn and his issue were to be 'adjudged English and . . . in every
manner as the king's subjects'.[25] Thereafter Kildare's interventions
in Tír Eoghain's politics became regular, supporting Conn's claim
to the succession and bringing increasingly powerful military
resources to bear against his O'Donnell-backed rivals; and over the
next four decades successfully imposing his own nominess –
Domhnall (1498–1509), Art Óg (1513–19) and Conn Bacach
(1519–59) – as the O'Neill. Geraldine influence in Tír Eoghain
was consolidated by layers of marriage alliances which ensured
that every O'Neill acquired powerful factional connections throughout the island and enabled them to re-establish sustained dynastic
stability, to withstand the rise of the O'Donnells, and to reassert
their dominance over the lesser lordships of Maguire, O'Reilly and
MacMahon. But it was also dangerous.[26]

It issued first in a major increase in the scale and character of violence in the region as the Geraldines brought ever larger forces with more modern weapons to bear against dissident interests in Ulster. Even more seriously, the very centre of the alliance was far from secure itself. In the early sixteenth century the power and independence of the Geraldines was fast becoming a source of mounting anxiety to the new Tudor monarchs Henry VII and Henry VIII, both of whom made fitful attempts to control them by their periodic displacement or subordination to constraining orders.[27] On these occasions it was incumbent on the O'Neills to offer support by fomenting trouble in Ulster and in the Pale in a manner designed to demonstrate the indispensability of the Geraldines to the peace of Ireland.[28] The risks entailed in such a game of bluff were always high; and in the crisis years of the early 1530s, when Henry VIII moved decisively against the Geraldines to enforce their conformity to his political and religious reforms, the O'Neills' bluff was eventually called. When Lord Offaly rebelled, Conn Bacach sent troops and stirred up trouble in south Ulster. But once it became clear that the crown was determined to suppress the rebellion, his support faltered; and even before Offaly surrendered, Conn had already made his peace with Lord Deputy Skeffington, renouncing Kildare, taking an oath of allegiance, and promising to make good damage done by his followers in the course of the rebellion.[29]

The most stable era of O'Neill rule in Ulster had thus come to an end. And now, bereft of a powerful national ally, surrounded on all sides by enemies, and having apparently exhausted all of the strategies of obtaining internal stability by means of diplomacy, Conn Bacach was obliged to go in search of yet another means of resolving the problems of O'Neill lordship.

REFORM

O'Neill's appreciation of the gravity of his situation is evidenced in the terms of the agreement made with Lord Deputy Grey in 1536 in which he again swore allegiance, promised compensation for losses, and renounced all claims to black rents on the Pale.[30] But despite such signs of goodwill, a fundamental obstacle to any rapprochement lay in the fact that, unlike the Geraldines, the new governor lacked the power to offer reciprocal support for such concessions and was in fact weaker than almost any of his predecessors.

Grossly under-resourced for the nationwide problems confronting him in the wake of the Kildare rebellion, Grey could do little other than demand concessions that he could do little to enforce. His weakness made Conn Bacach's task in sustaining a loyalist stance in Ulster all the harder, and O'Neill's difficulty was deepened by the diplomatic coup conducted by his cousin Lady Eleanor Fitzgerald, whose unexpected marriage to Manus O'Donnell had the effect of converting Conn's arch-enemy into a leader of the Geraldine cause.[31] Conn Bacach was thus presented with the choice, either to realign himself with the Geraldine confederacy to save the Kildare heir, or, in the hope of strengthening his vice-regal connections, to remain aloof from powerful Geraldine interests throughout the country. Thus pressed, he joined the Geraldine league, but continued to negotiate with Grey, hinting at a surrender of the young Kildare in return for recognition.[32] Conn's vacillation during this period, accounted for by historians merely as an expression of his natural deviousness, was in fact the only strategy available to him in very delicate circumstances: a recognition on his part that in the wake of the Kildare collapse he must make new terms with the crown, but that he could not abandon his old allies until the government's strength was sufficient to justify the move.

Grey's surprise ambush of a party of Conn's forces unprepared for attack from this quarter at Bellahoe in 1539 is evidence of O'Neill's genuine vulnerability at this time.[33] But two developments in the following year held out prospects of relief. The first was the decision of Lady Eleanor Fitzgerald to have the young Kildare heir sent abroad for safekeeping, thus removing the immediate Geraldine pressure on O'Neill. The second was the sudden fall of Grey in a palace coup against Thomas Cromwell and his replacement as deputy by one of the coup's beneficiaries, Sir Anthony St Leger.[34]

At the outset of his service St Leger appeared to have little else in mind toward the O'Neill other than a continuation of the aggressive strategy promoted by Grey in the aftermath of Bellahoe. Three rapid forays into Ulster, including a surprise attack in the middle of winter, appeared, according to St Leger's own account, to have had the effect of bringing Conn Bacach to his knees and forcing him to sue for peace.[35] But Conn was never actually confronted by St Leger, and when O'Neill eventually offered to submit late in 1541, the terms on which he negotiated were remarkably high. Upon making a full submission to King Henry and seeking pardon for all his past crimes, Conn sued with St Leger's support to be accepted as the crown's principal subject in Ulster, to have the status and provincial authority of the earls of Ormond and Desmond, and to have his equality with those senior peers formally recognised by his creation as the earl of Ulster.[36]

Such an explicit claim to provincial superiority was unprecedented, and it might seem strange that an English governor had accepted and even encouraged it. But behind the terms of Conn's submission there lay a radical initiative undertaken by St Leger under the framework of the Kingdom of Ireland Act (1541) by which the crown effectively abandoned the old lordship of Ireland and the fiction of a continuing war of conquest that went with it,

and offered instead a new constitution within which all the
inhabitants of Ireland would be regarded as equal subjects under a
common Irish sovereign.[37]

The attractions to Conn Bacach of such an initiative in the wake
of the Geraldine collapse were immense. For the new constitution
not only offered O'Neill the recognition which his predecessors
had long sought, but did so at a time when, bereft of allies and
surrounded by enemies, Conn Bacach urgently needed it. To clinch
the deal, however, it was necessary to make further concessions, to
which Conn hastily acceded. Thus in addition to his now familiar
offers to restrain his followers and to pay compensation for losses,
he agreed further to submit his current disputes with O'Donnell
concerning territory in Inishowen and Cinéal Moen and his more
general claims over the lesser lordships to arbitration and determination by royal commission.[38] He conceded also that he should not
have the title of 'Ulster' (which King Henry refused to yield) and
accepted instead the novel and lesser title of 'Tyrone'.[39] And he
agreed, finally, to formalise these terms through the surrender of
all his rights and the formal re-creation of his status and of his
dynastic succession in an elaborate ceremony conducted before
King Henry at Greenwich in the autumn of 1542.[40]

O'Neill had little difficulty in meeting these terms. Indeed, he
regarded the visit to court and the reconstitution of his dynasty
under English law as essential to his immediate survival. In nomi-
nating his heir, Feardorcha, whose right to succeed was explicitly
stated in separate letters patent ennobling him as the baron of
Dungannon, Conn Bacach also did not hesitate. His eldest son,
Feardorcha had been a loyal and effective lieutenant during the
crisis years of the 1530s, while his other sons were either rebellious
or, like Shane, too young to be of service. Feardorcha, it was true,
was a son born out of wedlock and received into Conn's household
when he was already grown. But in the revolutionary years of the

early 1540s, given the catastrophe that had just been averted and the great prospects that beckoned, such reservations as might have been raised about his choice as heir apparent mattered little. Yet within a decade, and in circumstances that could hardly have been foreseen in 1542, nothing else would matter at all.

CHAPTER 3

The Resistible Rise of Shane O'Neill, c.1530–56

Shane O'Neill's rise to become the most powerful war-lord in Ulster was far from inevitable. For the circumstances of his early life were obscure and quite unpromising. Even the manner in which his date of birth can be estimated is an indication of his uncertain beginnings. He was born either shortly before or some-time during 1530, when the annalists report that his mother, Sorcha, daughter of Hugh O'Neill, the chief of Clandeboy, died.[1]

Left motherless while in infancy, Shane was fostered out to the O'Donnellys, economically a moderately comfortable family whose status was enhanced by the fact that its head conveniently enjoyed the office of marshal to the O'Neill as an hereditary right.[2] Fosterage was common among Gaelic noble families, but it was not automatic. It was most frequently used as an attempt to cement diplomatic and military alliances; but the fostering out of supernumerary siblings to other houses was also employed to diffuse internal tensions within the families of lords who had many sons by dif-ferent marriages.[3] Conn Bacach's decision to send out Shane not to some potential ally or enemy, nor even to his mother's relatives, but to a lesser dependent family suggests that it was the latter consideration that was uppermost in his mind. In any case, it is clear that by the time of Shane's birth Conn was already a much-married man with several older sons to his name.

Although he always insisted that he was Conn Bacach's eldest legitimate son, Shane was not in fact even an elder member of the ruling family, but rather the youngest of at least five acknowledged sons.[4] The eldest, Feardorcha, was the most controversial. Shane, notoriously, charged that he was not an O'Neill at all, but the son of Alison and John Kelly, a blacksmith of Dundalk, who was acknowledged by Conn as his offspring only as a matter of honour. The circumstantial details repeated in Shane's various rehearsals of this story are sufficiently consistent and subject to contemporary validation to carry conviction.[5] But the suggestion that the O'Neill had been duped into accepting an imposter as his son is less plausible. For no one else ever questioned Conn's paternity; and Conn from early on granted Feardorcha senior status in the family. By the early 1540s Feardorcha was recognised by English and Irish observers as one of the principal powers in Tír Eoghain, and in the major treaties of 1541–2 his nomination as baron of Dungannon and heir to the earldom of Tyrone was accepted on all sides without controversy or comment.[6]

In 1541, then, the matter of Feardorcha's origin was not an issue; but even if it had been, there existed at least four other sons of O'Neill older than Shane whose legitimacy was in no doubt. After 1542 the eldest of this group, Felim Caoch, posed no obstacle to Shane's ambitions because he was killed in a skirmish with the MacDonnells. But three more sons, Turlough, Brian and Conn, whose recorded activities in the 1540s make clear that they were senior to Shane, were known to have been alive long after he first raised his claims to the succession.[7] In the scant records of Tír Eoghain's history in these years it is these men who receive notice. In the political surveys of the lordship drawn up as a preliminary to the surrender and regrant settlements of 1542 most of them are noted as men possessing 'fair countries'; but Shane is not mentioned. In the pardons preceeding the final treaty all are included, but not Shane. And in the formal indenture with the crown Shane is ignored because, as Campion observed, he 'was but a boy and not of much hope'.[8]

During these years of rapid change Shane, then, remained in obscurity, a younger son with far more influential older brothers, and probably still in the care of his foster-family. How long he remained with the O'Donnellys is uncertain, but the depth of his attachment to them is undoubted. At the very height of his powers in the mid-1560s, an English intelligence agent could still observe that Shane placed his trust 'not in the nobles of his country . . . not in his kinsmen or brothers. But wholly he assureth himself upon the safety of his foster-brothers'.[9] And within his own lifetime he was known to the Gaelic Irish not as 'Seán an Díomais', but as 'Seán Donnghaileach'.[10]

The highly unfavourable circumstances of Shane's early life make the speed of his rise to power among the O'Neills all the more difficult to understand. For here was no rightful heir to the lordship undoing a great wrong by reasserting his claim to the patrimony, but the quite unexpected triumph of one of the least advantaged players in an extremely dangerous game. Yet concerning the speed and decisiveness of his success there can be no doubt. In 1548 (aged 19 or 20) Shane first appears suddenly as a significant figure leading an expedition against the O'Neills of Clandeboy during which he killed the son of the lord.[11] In raiding Clandeboy, Shane went about his father's business, asserting O'Neill's traditional rights in the region. But by 1551 his independence was clear. In that year Tír Eoghain was convulsed by civil war among the sons of Conn Bacach. Conn himself had fled, and while seeking refuge in the Pale was arrested by agents of the Dublin government.[12] In his absence, the lordship's corn and cattle were laid waste and its people decimated by famine.

The principal fomentor of the war and the man responsible for its worst excesses was, it was widely reported, Shane himself.[13] And it was Shane who, by the close of 1552, had emerged as its only beneficiary. By then Conn Bacach was already a spent force and was released only in the hope that his return to Ulster might exercise some constraint over Shane, his 'youngest son', whom no one else could hope to influence.[14] At the same time the status of the baron of Dungannon was fatally damaged. Having bungled an opportunity to confront and destroy Shane, his authority in the lordship had dwindled, and by the closing months of 1552 he could depend on no more than 18 horsemen for protection.[15] The prospects of the remaining elder sons had similarly waned. Conn disappears entirely from the record, and seems likely to have perished in the wars.[16] Turlough sued for peace with Dublin, and seems thereafter to have depended wholly on the crown.[17] Brian's fate was more ignominious: he last appears being surrendered to Dublin as a hostage for the future good behaviour of Shane himself.[18] By the close of 1552 Dublin had come to recognise Shane's political dominance as a practical reality. Although he had several times broken a truce made with him in October 1551 and openly refused to support the crown in its efforts against the invading Scots in the north-east, no serious attempt was made against him. And with the return of Sir Anthony St Leger as viceroy in 1553, Shane's position as the government's favoured successor to the O'Neillship was confirmed by the award of a generous pension of 6s 8d a day.[19]

The extent of Shane's success in these few years thus emerges clearly even in the scant records of the period. But the causes underlying his achievement are less easily discovered. Personal characteristics – boldness, intelligence, ruthlessness – no doubt counted, but in what precise way can never be known. Yet it is possible to discern a number of external conditions which contributed strongly to the shaping of the environment in which he acted. The first of such factors lay in the implications of the surrender and regrant agreement which began to work themselves out in the decade after 1542. The attractions to Conn Bacach of surrender and regrant were, as we have seen, manifold. Reform promised serious long-term benefits; but it was its short-term value in the uncertain world of post-Geraldine Ulster politics that persuaded him to make concessions to the crown and his neighbours that he might not otherwise have yielded.

One such concession concerned the disputed lordship of Inishowen. Practical authority over the peninsula had long been enjoyed by the O'Donnells, but the O'Neills had regularly revived their claim by invasion and through the covert support of O'Donnell enemies among the O'Gallaghers. In 1542, however, Conn agreed to recognise the O'Donnell claim and to cease all further interventions in return for an annual payment of sixty cows. No provision was made as to how this rent was to be collected and O'Donnell defaulted (he seems never to have paid at all). Conn mounted a raid in distraint for his due in a manner that had been explicitly prohibited by the terms of the treaty, and was directed by the crown to return his spoils. Conn's discomfiture was deepened by a further conflict over the strategic castle of Lifford. Built by Siobhán O'Neill (Conn's sister and wife of Manus O'Donnell) on O'Neill territory, the castle had been given by her to her son Hugh. Manus disagreed and claimed it for the chieftaincy. Lifford thus became a centre of dispute between O'Donnell and O'Neill throughout the 1540s until Manus brusquely expelled Hugh and installed his preferred son Calvagh in 1549. O'Neill complained on behalf of Hugh but the Dublin government, as in the case of Inishowen, upheld O'Donnell's right to dispose of the castle as he saw fit.[20]

These troubles were accompanied by a number of similar conflicts with the lesser lords of Ulster arising out of the expectations provoked by surrender and regrant. The tenurial independence of Maguire, O'Reilly and MacMahon as subjects of the crown had been affirmed in the 1542 agreements, but complicated details remained unresolved. The question of outstanding debts owed by the lords to Conn was not addressed, the complex matter of acknowledged feudal obligations was left for future arbitration, the status of dependent families such as the O'Hanlons and the O'Cahans was not considered, and, most seriously of all, the actual treaties finally establishing the relationship of these lords with the crown were never drafted. In the later 1540s all of these matters became the source of intense wrangling between O'Neill and the lords as debts remained unpaid, obligations were extorted and factional intrigues between O'Neill and discontented figures in the lordships proliferated; and Dublin, though unwilling to settle the specific issues definitively, typically took the side of the lesser lords.[21]

The government's interim arbitrations did little to alter the course of politics in Ulster: the raids and counter-raids continued. But Conn's perceived recalcitrance in Dublin did much to diminish his credit as a friend of reform. More seriously, such persistent losses in relation to the old provincial enemies exacerbated his troubles in quarters closer to home. In 1542 his acceptance of the title of earl of Tyrone had led to the revolt of his then *tánaiste*, Niall Connallach. Niall's challenge was cut short by his sudden (unexplained) death in 1544.[22] At that time Niall's son, Turlough Luineach, was still too young to replace his father, but by the late 1540s he had begun staking his own claim and, more ominously, allying with the O'Donnells in their raids on Tír Eoghain.[23] A simultaneous threat, hardly less serious, came from Armagh, from the O'Neills of the Fews, a family of a type that was becoming increasingly common in sixteenth-century Ireland. The descendants of recent chieftains, these O'Neills had renounced any serious interest in the competition for the chieftainship, but they were determined to uphold their independence of all such claimants.[24] Their territorial independence had been explicitly recognised in 1542, but the details of their remaining obligations were never worked out. And throughout the 1540s Tyrone and Dungannon were engaged jointly in a campaign against the leader of the family, Felim Rua, to extract what they believed to be their residual rights of lordship.[25]

One final problem, concerning the O'Neills of Clandeboy, seemed hardly more significant. Yet it turned out to be the most critical. The treatment of the Clandeboy O'Neills under the terms of surrender and regrant was similar to that given to the other lesser lordships in Ulster, and relations between them and the O'Neill were correspondingly troubled. On the surface, the difficulty posed by the Clandeboy group was not of itself severe, because they were engaged in a bitter internecine war which rendered them powerless. Yet by their very weakness they presented the most grave threat to Conn Bacach's position, through their surrender to an external force just as powerful as the O'Neill himself. That force issued from the MacDonnells of the Isles.[26]

The intervention of the Scots in Ulster's politics was long-founded. But in the middle of the sixteenth century, with the collapse of the MacDonnells' own lordship in the Western Isles, the character of their influence changed decisively. For Ulster, rather than Scotland, now became the primary focus of the MacDonnells. They began appearing in massive expeditions – often in bands of 2,000 fighting men. But worse, they began to expand from the small pockets they had inhabited on the north coast, through the Glens and the Route and penetrating into the heartland of Antrim and even north Down, sweeping before them the small Gaelic and Anglo-Norman families of the area and undermining everywhere the overlordship of Clandeboy O'Neills.[27]

For Conn Bacach the disintegration of Clandeboy was deeply troubling. For although he might rejoice in the suffering of his enemies, he could not witness the present power struggle without being drawn to take sides. The knowledge that his enemies in Ulster would seek to exploit the opportunity made such involvement desirable; but the realisation that the Scots might establish themselves as a principal power in the province next to O'Neill made it a necessity. The Scots, however, were a source of extreme anxiety not simply to O'Neill, but also to his increasingly suspicious former friends in Dublin. And their ill-judged response to this common danger had the effect of increasing Conn's troubles immeasurably.

The significance of what was happening in north-east Ulster was misunderstood and exaggerated both in Dublin and at the English court. In Whitehall the embattled government of Protector Somerset believed that the MacDonnells' movement had been deliberately provoked by the French-dominated Edinburgh government as a means of opening a second front in France's larger conflict with England. This assumption was erroneous; but coupled with the (equally unfounded) fear that the French were planning an invasion of their own in the south of Ireland, it prompted a sudden reversal of priorities in the formulation of English policy for Ireland. It was now decided that the halting, flexible diplomacy that had characterised the late Henrician years should, for the present at least, be superseded by a greater vigilance and a greater show of strength through the construction of new coastal defences, the refurbishment of existing forts and the extension of small garrisons throughout the country. The grander ambitions of this Edwardian programme were never realised – the great coastal defences were never built. But in regard to the north important changes occurred. There a small group of professional soldiers were introduced as garrison commanders in strategic places with authority to stem the inflow of Scots and discourage those in Ulster who might be tempted to ally with them.[28]

The most important of such figures was Nicholas Bagenal, a Staffordshire man with a violent and dubious past who was appointed marshal of the army in 1547, sent north by Lord Deputy Bellingham in 1549, and granted the extensive property of the monastery of Newry on generous terms as a base from which to co-ordinate the English presence in Ulster.[29] Bagenal was supported by his brother Ralph, appointed by Bellingham under controversial circumstances to the ward at Carrickfergus. A third was Andrew Brereton, who was appointed constable in Lecale, and a fourth was Roger Brooke, appointed to the castle of Dundrum.[30] The ability of these men to influence the events that were taking place in Ulster was, given the size of the forces involved, quite limited. Yet precisely because of their vulnerability, they pursued a strategy of sustained aggression toward the Ulster Irish, and in particular toward O'Neill. The Bagenals raided Tír Eoghain on several occasions, taking massive spoils and, in one instance, singling out for special punishment Shane's foster-brothers, the O'Donnellys. Brooke and Brereton raided Conn's allies among the MacQuillans and in Iveagh. When Conn Bacach sent a force to MacCartan's country to collect rents, Brereton ambushed them, killing over 140 of his men, including Conn's wife's younger brothers. When Conn came to Dublin to protest against such actions, Brereton in company with Bagenal openly called him a traitor at the council table.[31]

This unchecked hostility reflected a marked change of attitude on the part of the English toward O'Neill. For hitherto Dublin, particularly under St Leger, had been anxious not to alienate Tyrone altogether. Thus even while government arbitrations between O'Neill and his neighbours generally found against O'Neill,

St Leger made sure that no punitive action was to be launched against Conn Bacach. He also took steps to ensure that the good faith between the king and the earl established by Conn's visit to Greenwich in 1542 was continued, organising a regular correspondence and exchange of gifts. Such diplomacy worked, and as late as 1545 Conn Bacach confirmed his continuing enthusiasm for his role as 'the king's friend' by organising and dispatching a large contingent of Ulster kerne to serve in King Henry's expedition to Boulogne.[32]

With St Leger's recall, all this changed as his successor, Bellingham, implemented Somerset's garrisoning policy in Ulster. But even on his return in 1550, St Leger proved unable to reverse what Bellingham had started. Thus he reopened negotiations with Conn Bacach, defended his actions against the garrisons, and sought to have the garrison commanders themselves dismissed. But in each case he was overruled by Whitehall. His defence of Conn Bacach was rebuked, his attempts to appoint new men in Ulster were overturned, and in less than a year St Leger himself was recalled, leaving Conn's English enemies in Ulster free to continue their harassment of Tír Eoghain.[33]

Thus in the middle of 1551 Conn Bacach determined to act alone. Abandoned and even threatened by the one political force on which in the 1540s he had placed so much hope, he moved to reassert O'Neill's authority in Ulster in the traditional way, with no further consideration for the consequences. He began war close to home, attacking his own sons, Conn, Turlough and Brian, whose ambitions to succeed to their father's place had been whetted by his failures in the recent past. He rounded next on Turlough Luineach, silencing his aspirations to be recognised as *tánaiste*. But he then launched an unexpected attack on Dublin's man, Feardorcha, the baron of Dungannon. This last action precipitated a complicated three-cornered war in which Dungannon (aided by

Bagenal and the other English captains), the remaining elder sons (drawing support from the O'Donnells and the O'Neills of Clandeboy), and Conn Bacach himself all independently confronted each other.[34]

Although he could count on the loyalty of the chieftain's traditional military retainers, Conn Bacach enjoyed no support from within the ruling family except from the younger, and hitherto discounted Shane. And it was this contrast between his immediate military strength and his deeper political and diplomatic weakness that persuaded St Leger's replacement in 1551, Sir James Croft, acting on the advice of Bagenal and of the lord chancellor, Sir Thomas Cusack, to risk the arrest of Conn Bacach and to encourage Dungannon to make war on all the remaining O'Neills.[35] The arrest was efficiently executed, but it served only to define the real issues at stake in the O'Neills' civil war. Dungannon, inevitably identified by all concerned with the side that had imprisoned the chieftain, and believed by many to have been ultimately responsible for his arrest, immediately lost support throughout the lordship and soon found himself wholly dependent on the swords of the English captains. At the same time more temperate allies of the crown, like O'Neill of the Fews, MacMahon and even O'Reilly, frightened or embarrassed by the action also withdrew support, so that Bagenal and the other English forces in Ulster could do little to influence developments, except to survive. Dungannon's disappearance did more than simplify the contest. For the government's action had also had the simultaneous effect of catapulting into prominence the one figure not associated with any of the sides that had brought Conn Bacach so low – his 'youngest son' Shane.

Almost immediately on Conn Bacach's arrest Shane staked his claim to be the protector of the O'Neill lordship by a ceremonial visit to Dungannon to take possession of the O'Neill treasury for safekeeping until the chief returned.[36] The symbolism of the action was unmistakable, and Shane followed it through by sending messengers to the nobility of Ireland, informing them of the plight of the dynasty. On no occasion, however, did he make any claim to be Conn Bacach's successor, but acted merely as his representative, assuming temporary responsibility for the lordship in a time of crisis. Shane's determination to be seen as the man 'most likely to follow his father's conduct' was sufficiently persuasive to cause the Dublin government to contemplate his arrest also.[37] But as yet the real political influence of this late arrival remained uncertain. Although considerations of loyalty and fear of chronic war might have inclined many among the leading families of Tír Eoghain to look sympathetically on Shane, few were willing directly to attach themselves to him at the outset. But the longer Shane survived as an independent agent, the more legitimacy his position acquired. What Shane urgently needed in order to establish himself, there-fore, was an autonomous fighting force of sufficient strength to overwhelm the armies of his feuding brothers and thus to alter the calculations of the wavering lesser families in the lordship. And once again at this critical moment the opportunity was provided to him by the decisive, but quite ill-considered, actions of the government in Dublin.

Following his arrest of Tyrone, Lord Deputy Croft proceeded directly to embark on one of the principal obligations of his official instructions, a campaign to expel the MacDonnells.[38] At first, as was typical of expeditions of this kind, success seemed assured. The Scots melted away and their supporters either fled or, like Hugh MacNeill Óg of Clandeboy, hurried to submit. But the actual effect of Croft's military adventure was to bring about nothing less than a diplomatic revolution in Ulster. Formerly the relationship between the chief of the O'Neills and the colonising Scots (and their Irish allies) was unquestionably hostile, for whatever use an O'Neill might have wished to make of Scots mercenaries from time to time, the prospect of their settling permanently as a major force in Ulster presented a grave challenge to the power of O'Neill. But in circumstances where both interests were experiencing simultaneous attack from a common source, the advantages of a realignment were obvious.

Again Shane was the one to seize the initiative. When Croft and his army arrived in Ulster seeking support for the campaign to repulse the Scots invader, most of the lords proffered aid, but Shane, despite his own vulnerability, pointedly did not. Evasive at first, he gradually became more open in his defiance, launching attacks on the rear of Croft's army, destroying supplies, raiding cattle and supplying advance intelligence on its movements to the Scots *via* their principal Irish ally, and first target of Croft's expedition, Hugh MacNeill Óg of Clandeboy.[39] On his own Hugh MacNeill was not a dominant figure in Ulster politics. A contender for the overlordship of Clandeboy, he was struggling for a prize that was diminishing in value with each passing day. Yet he had one crucial strength. He had allied with the Scots, and he was now using them to advance his claims, even though in the process they were laying waste to anything of value in Clandeboy. However incongruous it may have been in principle, an alliance between the rebel of Clandeboy, quisling to the Scots, and the representative of O'Neill brought immediate benefits to both parties. For Hugh, Shane's rearguard support was, in the face of his confrontation with Croft, vital; but Shane was also a prospective customer for his Scots, offering alternative employment to those troublesome allies who were in the process of devastating his inheritance. The foundation of their alliance, therefore, lay in their deployment of mercenary troops: desperately needed by Shane, and in oversupply with Hugh.

Thus it was through Hugh MacNeill that Shane got his independent fighting force at precisely the time he needed it; and he proceeded to employ it in a ruthless manner to enforce his conservative and legitimist claim. With his newly acquired Scots, Shane now radically transformed the civil war in Tír Eoghain, mercilessly destroying the crops and seizing the cattle of any who refused him total submission; he laid waste the lordship and spread famine everywhere. At the same time he openly defied the efforts of Bagenal and Cusack to bring about a lasting peace and renounced any intention of settling with Dublin until the traditional rights of the O'Neill in Tír Eoghain and throughout Ulster had been fully re-established.[40]

In bringing his war against all the forces that had depleted the power of the O'Neillship in the previous decade to a triumphant conclusion, Shane was again supported by the final collapse of Croft's anti-Scots policy in the summer of 1552. Having briefly retreated, the Scots returned in greater force than ever. In attempting to attack them and Hugh MacNeill at Belfast, Croft suffered heavy losses. Reinforcements from the baron of Dungannon were hastily called upon, but they were almost immediately ambushed by Shane and destroyed. Thus mauled, Croft abandoned his pursuit of Hugh MacNeill and hastened back to Dublin, where he immediately sued for recall.[41] Croft's defeat left Hugh MacNeill Óg unopposed in Clandeboy, and his ally Shane triumphant in Tír Eoghain. Belatedly recognising the failure of its Ulster policy, Dublin sued for peace on the only terms acceptable to Shane. Granting a full amnesty for all the depredations of the recent past, the crown simply required that pledges be sent for future good behaviour and agreed to the immediate restoration of Conn Bacach. Edward VI then wrote personally to Tyrone, assuring him of royal favour in a new round of arbitrations that Dublin was now about to initiate.[42] Behind this rapid reversal of government policy lay the hand of the old reformer of the early 1540s, St Leger, who was reappointed lord deputy in 1553.[43] St Leger's return to Ireland accelerated the process of reconciliation, promising a revision of the humiliating terms set by the arbitrations of the late 1540s, and recognising Shane as Conn Bacach's likely heir by means of a generous royal pension.[44]

By the middle of the 1550s, then, Shane, saviour of his patrimony, merciless scourge of his enemies, and now the new friend of the English government, had emerged as the most powerful figure in Gaelic Ulster. But certain obstacles to his complete triumph remained: some the results of the recent upheavals, but others of a deeper and more obstinate nature. His claims to have been the representative of his father entailed that once Conn Bacach had been restored to his legitimate place he could not readily be displaced by his own defender. And once restored, Conn Bacach began to assert himself against his younger son by turning again to his eldest, the baron of Dungannon. Dungannon was by now also a much-depleted force, but his status as Conn's nominated successor to the earldom granted the old man some options other than simply yielding to Shane. Shane's eventual succession to the chieftainship seemed inevitable, but his father's unwillingness to accept it meant that Shane had perforce to wait until death gave him by right what was already his in fact.[45]

This irksome hiatus in Shane's career was complicated by a second problem: his necessary but dangerous alliance with the Scots. Like any prospective O'Neill, Shane was anxious to distance himself from the invaders as quickly as possible, but he was now compelled to delay any definitive break until his father Conn Bacach yielded. Conn's conduct, indeed, even forced Shane to reaffirm his goodwill toward the MacDonnells. For on his return the old chief, in company with Dungannon, attempted to assert his authority by mounting an attack on the traditional enemy. To have allowed them a victory in this adventure was, of course, unthinkable; and the opportunity of exposing their empty pretensions was not to be ignored. So, as he had against Croft, Shane sided openly with the Scots and participated in the total rout of Conn Bacach's army which confirmed the chieftain's eclipse and ended whatever threat remained from his alliance with Dungannon.[46]

Alliance with the Scots once again worked to Shane's benefit. But in addition to the costs implicit in such continuing dependence, the relationship raised serious obstacles to Shane's attempt to establish good relations with Dublin. The returned viceroy St Leger was disposed to be tolerant of his intrigues. But the governor's own failure to do anything to stem the Scots settlement was a major source of discontent with his own administration at court. In this lay the last and most fundamental of Shane's difficulties: the instability and unpredictability of the English administration in Ireland. The disruption of St Leger's previous viceroyalties was the principal cause of the wars that had broken out in Ulster in the early 1550s. And when in the summer of 1556 St Leger was finally recalled, not least because of his failure against the Scots, the major bulwark that had allowed Shane to bide his time in relative calm until the succession became his was now removed. Then, like his father before him, Shane was left to confront a new administration, under the leadership of the untried but ambitious earl of Sussex, with whom he had no personal links. Thus he moved with renewed urgency to consolidate his position.

CHAPTER 4

The Lost Peace, 1556–62

Shane's escape from the uncertainties which afflicted him in the mid-1550s was speedy but not without cost. Among the O'Neills, following the discomfiture of the earl and Dungannon against the Scots, he steadily reinforced his authority, securing submissions from the principal families of the lordship and forcing Felim Rua O'Neill of the Fews, his only serious opponent among this group, to flee his territory and seek refuge in the Pale.[1] Towards the south Shane was more overtly aggressive, raiding Maguire, O'Reilly and MacMahon in punishment for their refusal to yield what he claimed to be his rightful tribute. Thus he steadily closed the circle on Conn Bacach and Dungannon, until in 1558 he finally rid himself of his rival for the earldom by having Dungannon assassinated. After Dungannon's murder Conn Bacach fled from Tír Eoghain, seeking sanctuary in the house of the bishop of Meath (William Walsh), where he died helpless early in 1559.[2] On his death, Shane proceeded immediately to have himself installed as the O'Neill on the ancient inauguration stone at Tullaghogue in a great ceremony witnessed by a huge assembly of the lordship's inhabitants.[3]

In this success Shane was aided by two external contingencies. One was the collapse of Tír Conaill into dynastic war precipitated by the usurpation of the chieftainship by Calvagh O'Donnell, which neutralised opposition from that quarter.[4] The second was the sudden death of Hugh MacNeill Óg of Clandeboy in 1555, which enabled Shane to establish a direct relationship with the MacDonnells.[5] These developments eased Shane's path to Tullaghogue; but coupled with the violence he had displayed against Dungannon and Tyrone, they also earned for him the grave suspicion of the new viceroy, the earl of Sussex.

Sussex was at the outset an unknown quantity who had pledged himself to the spirit of surrender and regrant, but who came also with a substantially increased army and a marked intolerance for dissent. Shane's approach was, therefore, cautious. Shortly after Sussex's arrival Shane formally submitted and received a general pardon for past misdeeds. In 1557, however, when Sussex went north, demanding that the Ulster chiefs aid him in another attempt to expel the Scots, Shane proved evasive, guiding the campaign army safely through Tír Eoghain, but excusing himself from the train before the Scots were engaged.[6] In 1558, when Sussex renewed the offensive, Shane behaved similarly; but his dissimulation could no longer be cloaked. On neither occasion was there any evidence that Shane had actually aided the Scots as he had in the past, and between the two campaigns he sought to reassure the crown by negotiating on friendly terms with Sussex's deputy, Sir Henry Sidney, whom he invited to stand as godfather to one of his children.[7]

Yet for all that, Sussex himself had become convinced of Shane's fundamental disloyalty and reacted accordingly, launching in 1557 a violent attack on Armagh and allowing the cathedral, its treasury and the adjacent chapels to be looted at will by his soldiers. The raid was, characteristically, intended by Sussex to be exemplary; but by its very violence – the city itself remained a ruin for most of the century – it simply had the effect of poisoning relations between O'Neill and the governor permanently.[8]

It was in these unhappy circumstances that Shane became the O'Neill and immediately sued the crown to succeed to his father's title as earl of Tyrone. Queen Elizabeth's initial response was positive. In view of the fact that Shane was

> the eldest son legitimate of the earl of Tyrone . . . we think it more meet, especially for the preferment of the person legitimate in blood and next that he is thereof in quiet possession that the deputy shall allow him to succeed to his father.[9]

But the actual negotiations which were supposed to give effect to this decision in principle turned out to be disastrous. Conducted in September 1559 in an atmosphere of extreme mistrust – Shane insisted that the most senior figures in Sussex's administration be handed over as pledges before he would come to the governor – they foundered on two matters quite extraneous to the central issue: Shane's insistence that restitution be made for his losses at Armagh, and Sussex's refusal to confer the title of earl on Shane until all of Shane's disputes with the lesser lords of Ulster and the major families of Tír Eoghain had been settled by government arbitration. The talks ended angrily and Sussex provided his own heavily weighted account of Shane's demeanour during the negotiations to persuade Elizabeth to the option which he had favoured all along – war.[10]

From the beginning, however, Sussex's war plans were fraught with difficulty. Depending primarily on the construction of a grand alliance among the Ulster lords against O'Neill, his effort faltered when Shane marched through the southern lordships of Ulster in August 1560 with a massive force, and the great confederation melted away. Through the winter of 1560–1 Sussex worked again to reconstruct his alliance and to keep his reinforced English army on a war-footing. By May 1561 he was at last ready to fight, and he printed a proclamation detailing all of the evils Shane had committed since 1556 as a public declaration of war. But this time

Shane's pre-emptive action was decisive. Sometime toward the end of May he seized Calvagh O'Donnell and his wife and took them prisoner to Dungannon. The alliance once again began to crumble. But Shane delivered the *coup de grâce* when he surprised and routed the rearguard of Sussex's English army as it proceeded through Armagh. The defeat ended Sussex's war before it had hardly begun, and for the first time the government in Whitehall began to look seriously at the alternative approach which Shane and his agents had been promoting since the failure of the talks back in September 1559.[11]

Since then, O'Neill through the earl of Kildare and Terence Donnelly, the dean of Armagh, had been seeking to present his own case in person to Whitehall, promising to allow his differences with other parties in Ulster to be adjudicated upon by the crown at the point of his accession to the title of Tyrone. The proposal clearly echoed Conn Bacach's submission to King Henry twenty years earlier, and in making it Shane was deliberately affirming his continuing enthusiasm for the policy of surrender and regrant. Yet when it was first raised by Dean Donnelly and Kildare in 1560, it was coldly received. And it was only after the calamitous failure of the war policy in the summer of 1561, and a bungled attempt by Sussex to have Shane assassinated, that Secretary Cecil and the rest of the English council began to take the prospect of O'Neill's visit seriously.[12] In tortuous negotiations conducted at the close of 1561 almost all of Shane's conditions concerning his personal safety and the security of his lands were met, and Shane even succeeded in extracting a massive loan of £2,000 from the parsimonious Elizabeth to enable him to deport himself in an appropriately noble manner.[13]

His reception at court seemed, moreover, to confirm his success. He was entertained by such senior councillors as Secretary Cecil, Lord Keeper Bacon and the earl of Pembroke. He was taken up by the favourite Lord Robert Dudley, who entertained him lavishly

and supplied his own clients, Sir Henry Sidney and Thomas
Stucley, to act as his companions. Shane too began to expend his
allowance on entertaining and was reported to have made quite an
impression, adopting the dress and deportment of a courtier.[14]
When he came to make his formal appearance before Elizabeth on
the 6 January 1562, the diplomatic advantage appeared also to
remain with Shane. He was received by Elizabeth early, before Lord
Lieutenant Sussex, who had pleaded to be heard first. His submission was complete; but it was also short and delivered in Irish by
Shane, who had resumed his native costume for the occasion and
entered surrounded by his ceremonially armed galloglass – only
later was an English text delivered quietly to Elizabeth and her
council.[15]

The case which Shane then proceeded to make seemed formidable. First he argued that Dungannon's illegitimacy rendered his
nomination as successor to the earldom wholly invalid. The original
treaty was therefore null, and ought to be renegotiated from the
beginning on the same terms that had been agreed with Conn
Bacach. He next claimed that, since he alone had succeeded to the
title of O'Neill, both by inheritance and through election by his
people, the earldom could be conferred on him alone. Shane
stressed this point not only because of its intellectual coherence,
but also because of its practical advantage. His claim to elected
status was one which neither Dungannon nor his sons could ever
have made, and was designed to reinforce the queen's initial
preference for the one who was already 'in quiet possession' of his
country. Shane's case therefore seemed strong; but when Sussex
arrived at court in February, O'Neill found himself confronted
with an unexpected challenge.[16]

For all its great ceremony and expressions of mutual trust, the
settlement of 1542–3, Sussex argued, was not an agreement among
equals, as Shane seemed to presume, but simply the full submission

of the rebel Conn Bacach O'Neill to his rightful sovereign, whose rights over Ulster – both as king and lord of Ireland and as heir to the earldom of Ulster – had long been usurped, most especially by the O'Neills. The elevation of Conn Bacach to the status of an earl was a matter of the crown's grace and political convenience; it was not a contract. And although it was true that the queen might choose to invalidate the grant if she judged that Conn Bacach had acted in bad faith in concealing Dungannon's illegitimacy, that decision would have nothing to do with Shane's case, and Shane's own claim to be the elected O'Neill had in principle nothing to do with that decision.[17]

To all of this Shane and his advisers had prepared an answer. It was not merely as an individual that Conn Bacach had submitted to the crown in 1542, but as the 'officer' and representative of the O'Neills, his people. For it was only as such that he could have given the wide-ranging undertakings that he gave concerning the reform of the lordship. In submitting in this way, he was, moreover, merely reiterating, though in a far more elaborate manner, the oath of fealty which several of his predecessors as O'Neill had sworn to the earls of Ulster, whose title rights and obligations had now descended by inheritance to the house of Tudor. Thus, both in terms of historical and legal precedent and in terms of the constitutional relationship of the O'Neill to his people, it was clear that the 1542 settlement had been intended to be made not with some casual individual in an accidental position of power, but with the 'officer' of the O'Neills. The validity of this interpretation of the original agreement, Shane went on to claim in a manner which seemed to clinch the case, was confirmed by the inclusion both in the indentures of surrender and in the indentures of regrant of rights which belonged to Conn Bacach not as an individual, but had been derived from obligations he had assumed as 'the O'Neill'. These moves in 1542 may or may not have been inadvertent – there was no one who could tell – and Shane gave a clear indication that he was willing to negotiate away these particular rights in any new settlement that might be arrived at by the close of the current negotiations. But the terms of the original treaty signed and sealed with all due ceremony could not simply be abrogated and could only be changed by the agreement of both parties, the crown and the O'Neill, and so it was time to start again with the current conciliatory, but undisputed, O'Neill.[18]

This was theoretically very clever, but perhaps too clever. For in making his point, Shane was also calling into question the legitimacy of all the similar settlements of surrender and regrant which had been made with Gaelic lords throughout the island since the 1540s. It was this dire implication that would eventually lead, as we have seen in chapter 1, to the grand historical revisions of the parliament of 1569, the statutory condemnation of the usurpations of 'the O's' and 'the Mac's', and the blackening of Shane's posthumous reputation as an impossible tyrant. This, however, was all in the future, and there is no reason to conclude that some means short of the radical measures of 1569 might have been attained, had there been goodwill on both sides. But trust and goodwill, already in short supply by 1562, were further diminished by the reaction of the opposing negotiators to Shane's *demarche*.

For however plausible they may have appeared in theory, Shane's claims regarding the rights that were directly attached to the O'Neillship rendered his negotiating position, in the short term at least, strategically vulnerable. The O'Neillship, Sussex retorted, though a political reality as far as Shane was concerned, had no standing in English law. Yet if any progress was to be made in coming to terms with Shane, it was imperative, given his stress on the importance of the office, that a number of questions concerning his understanding of the status of O'Neill should first be put to him before the crown considered looking again at the 1542 settlement at all. Thus rather than securing an answer to his suit for the earldom, Shane found himself faced with a set of questions concerning his claim to the O'Neillship through which the government sought to secure his acceptance of a highly limited definition of his presumed rights, as a precondition to any future negotiations concerning his possible candidacy for the earldom. Denying his claims over O'Donnell, O'Reilly, Maguire, and O'Neill of the Fews, they required that his controversies with them be settled by government arbitration. They demanded that he support the establishment of a provincial council in Armagh and prohibited him from imposing coyne and livery on any lands beyond his personal lordship.[19]

There was little in these demands themselves that was absolutely unacceptable in principle. For implicitly they recognised Shane's status as a major provincial figure, and conceded even some elements of feudal overlordship. Shane had, moreover, already agreed to the introduction of a council in Ulster, and asked only that in its initial stages its interpretation of law should not be so narrow as to undermine the ancient customs of the country, while the prohibition of coyne was moderated by a clause to the effect that O'Neill could make war without permission in the face of due provocation.[20]

But such room for manoeuvre as existed in theory was considerably narrowed by the crown's firm insistence that a clear definition of the entitlements of the O'Neill was a necessary prior condition to any further discussion concerning the earldom of Tyrone. And it was closed altogether by an additional royal decision, suggested by Secretary Cecil and presented to Shane at the close of March, that a final judgement in regard to the earldom would be made only when Elizabeth had first interviewed the heir of the late baron of Dungannon, his son Brian.[21] This last and late stipulation constituted a withdrawal from the terms of reference under which negotiations had been conducted with Shane since 1559. And as such it provided the clearest possible evidence to Shane that the crown had now ceased to negotiate in good faith. There is evidence that this abrupt changing of the terms of the negotiations was due on Cecil's part more to the secretary's primary concern with the preservation of his own active Anglo-Scottish policy, and his particular anxiety not to alienate the Scottish earl of Argyll, an old enemy of Shane's, in the complex Anglo-Scottish negotiations concerning the return of Mary, Queen of Scots which were taking place precisely at this time.[22] And Cecil may have seen his intervention primarily as a delaying tactic rather than an attempt to destroy the process altogether. Such an attitude seems most probably; for in reality this new requirement, like the previous attempt to force restrictive concessions from him under pressure, was quite unenforceable. For just as it was clear that Shane could never be held to concessions he believed were extracted from him by blackmail, it was equally obvious on the other side that the young Dungannon could make no serious claim to influence of any sort in Ulster.[23]

This practical weakness in the crown's negotiating position was quickly and brutally exposed when, in early April, young Dungannon was murdered. Shane, claiming innocence, reported that the outrage had been committed by a rebellious Turlough Luineach O'Neill, as part of an attempt to usurp the O'Neillship. Thus pleading the urgency of the situation in Ulster, Shane hastily signed the terms placed before him and sought immediate licence to return. With nothing left to bargain with and unable to detain him on any legal grounds, Elizabeth grudgingly conceded, and Shane hurried back to Ireland, frustrated, angry, and determined to make good his loss of authority in Ulster which had been the only real consequence of his long, and fruitless *sojourn* at court.[24]

The significance of the opportunities lost at court in the early months of 1562 can hardly be overstated. Immediate political costs were obvious. Failure, following such a major investment from both sides, seriously intensified mutual suspicion and ill-will and made future confrontation almost inevitable. But there were deeper costs. For the arguments had laid bare fundamental problems concerning the nature of the surrender process itself. Shane's identification of the O'Neill lordship with the earldom had been tactically disadvantageous in that it forced him to negotiate on practical details before he had won an agreement in principle. But it nevertheless represented a perfectly accurate restatement of the assumptions shared by both sides in the 1540s concerning the way in which their diplomacy must proceed. The precise details of lordship, the degree to which any particular chieftain was entitled to rights over the inhabitants of his country, were, it was then agreed, matters which should be subject to arbitration thereafter. But in rejecting this assumption and in affirming instead that they were a necessary precondition to the initiation of the process, Sussex and Cecil were enacting a profound reversal of policy. In overriding also the manifest flaws inherent in the 1542 agreement, and insisting on the primacy of royal authority even before the process of surrender had been undergone, they were in effect negating the significance of the surrender and regrant process itself. This was a radical departure; one frequently seen in retrospect as yet another instance of England's implacable hostility to the claims of the native Irish lords. But the roots of this *demarche* may be traced to sources at once more complex, more considered and also more contingent than has often been supposed.

The notion that Sussex was bent upon some grand strategy to conquer Ulster by force, though sometimes uncritically assumed by historians, has little foundation in fact. Sussex never avowed such an objective, and the forces allowed to him by the crown were never anything near enough for such a purpose. In 1560–1, at the height of his campaign against O'Neill, the number of troops directly under his command hardly exceeded 2,500. His war against O'Neill was, in fact, heavily dependent on local support – primarily from the Ulster lords – and it was the fragile nature of this assistance that caused his efforts so frequently to collapse. But for Sussex such alliance-making was not merely a matter of military exigency; it was a central part of his Ulster policy. In his most optimistic plans drawn up for Ulster for the time when Shane had been suppressed, he envisaged no extensive confiscations, nor even small colonising schemes. Rather he proposed the re-organisation of provincial society through the erection of local administrative units, headed by a provincial council, in which the power of the lords, including a scaled-down lord of Tír Eoghain, would be preserved and social and tenurial relations between the lords and their people would be clarified and standardised by trial at law. At the back of the conflict between Sussex and Shane there lay, then, no crude confrontation between the English conquistador and the native chief, but a question of how the O'Neill was to be fitted into the reformed and anglicised Ulster envisaged in the process of surrender and regrant.[25]

For St Leger and those who followed him, this question, though fraught with formidable problems in actual practice, was in principle relatively simple: the location of the O'Neill amidst the other sources of power in Ulster was merely a matter of painstaking and sustained compromise and arbitration. But for Sussex the O'Neill problem could not be treated in such a confined provincial way. He recognised that the size and internal divisions of the lordship had driven every O'Neill to seek allies on a national level, involving themselves in all sorts of affairs outside the province in order to secure greater internal stability, and in the sixteenth century their most powerful domestic allies in this strategy were the Fitzgeralds of Kildare. Seen from a longer perspective, therefore, the great initiatives of the 1540s had been conducted, according to Sussex, in a peculiar and quite artificial atmosphere during the crucial eclipse of the powerful Geraldines, and at a time when the O'Neill, surrounded by provincial enemies, was desperately in need of external allies. But now the Geraldines were back, since the restoration of Gerald Fitzgerald as 11th earl of Kildare in 1553–4. The reconstruction of the old Fitzgerald–O'Neill alliance was in process, and the resumption of uncontrolled O'Neill expansionism in Ulster under Shane was its clearest result. Thus, given the broader, national ramifications of the O'Neill recovery, it was imperative, Sussex believed, that the proponents of English reform in Ulster should revise both their analyses and their practices.[26]

Sussex had a point. For Kildare had been quick to attach Shane to his cause. As early as 1554 he was in Ulster supporting Shane against the lesser lords, while reviving the Geraldine title to the lordship of Lecale in County Down in opposition to the English settlers there. It was Kildare who brokered the first negotiations between Sussex and Shane in 1559, and who first suggested the idea of direct negotiations with the queen at court. When Sussex's failures in 1560–1 persuaded Elizabeth of the need for diplomacy, it was Kildare who was commissioned with the delicate task of setting the terms for the visit and organising the practical arrangements. And when Shane at last arrived before Elizabeth, it was Kildare who presented him to the queen.[27]

Kildare's intimate involvement with Shane's peace effort profoundly coloured Sussex's attitude toward the substance of the initiative itself. For the viceroy related it to his own quite original critique of conventional views of the problem of governing Ireland which he had worked out in a series of memoranda drafted between the late 1550s and 1562. That conventional approach, formulated

in the reformist tracts of the early decades of the century, and put
into operation in the heady days of the 1540s, had argued that the
fundamental cause of the island's lawlessness and poverty could be
traced to the nefarious system of extortions known summarily as
'coyne and livery'. 'Coyne and livery' was destroying everything,
the analysts claimed, and if a move was set on foot gradually to
dismantle the system, by means of the diplomatic process we know
as surrender and regrant, ever-increasing numbers of the native
powers would rapidly cleave to the government's cause until
coyne would at last wither away. But Sussex concluded that such
expectations were false, and had failed over the succeeding twenty
years because 'coyne and livery' was not the cause of the country's
decay, but the symptom, or rather the operating medium, of a
more complex political phenomenon which had organised all of
the forces in the lordships of Ireland into grand factions transcending and subordinating all other cultural and ethnic divides.
The influence exercised by these opposing factions was systemic,
dominating both regional and local politics. Thus the attempt to
dissolve 'coyne and livery' as a simple evil was doomed to fail either
because elements in both factions would resist it, or because one
side would seek to exploit the weakness of whoever had agreed to
accept reform. This, Sussex believed, was what Kildare and the
Geraldines were determined to do.[28]

    In challenging Shane and his diplomatic initiative, Sussex,
then, was confronting the Geraldines and mounting an attack on
their politics of faction which had undermined every English
attempt to reform the whole of the Irish lordships in the past.
Thus it was both as the symbol and the most powerful agent of
faction that Shane's provincial ambitions were at all costs to be
opposed. For his success in winning by his own terms would
validate not only the way he had seized power in Ulster but also the
ascendancy of the Geraldine faction all over the island. Thus for

Sussex, Shane's discomfiture was not simply a vendetta, but the test of English government in Ireland as a whole. There was, then, hardly any rhetorical exaggeration in the claim he had made to Elizabeth: 'If Shane be overthrown, all is settled; if Shane settle, all is overthrown.'[29]

By relating the politics of Ulster to the politics of faction in Ireland as a whole, Sussex believed he had offered sufficient justification for abandoning the simplistic conceptions of the 1540s and adopting a more radical approach toward the settlement of Ulster. But the cogency of his analysis would have counted for little with those for whom even the whole of Ireland featured only as a secondary and relatively distant problem had his preoccupation with faction not been immediately pertinent to the politics of Elizabeth's own court, and to the position of the queen's secretary, Sir William Cecil, in particular.

Of unmistakable importance in the political calculations of sixteenth-century Ireland, the significance of faction in Elizabethan England has been much downgraded by historians in recent years. For some its appearance was only intermittent and usually kept under control; for others it hardly existed at all, the heated contentions among Elizabeth's closest courtiers being merely the most vigorous expressions of a vibrant 'culture of counsel'.[30] Though far from receiving universal acceptance, this revisionist view has been considerably strengthened by its success in substituting for the older Namierite approach to history, an alternative perspective which has stressed the independent importance of ideological motives in determining political actions. In regard to Sir William Cecil in particular, Stephen Alford has argued that the secretary was not simply a court politician, holding his own among the competing interests of the established nobility and the party of the rising favourite, Lord Robert Dudley. He was instead a passionate Protestant ideologue, determined to defend the English Reformation against the challenges of ascendant Catholic forces in Europe. Central to this objective was the question of the Tudor succession. Cecil was resolved that Elizabeth should marry a Protestant prince, and failing in that he was no less determined that the succession of the Catholic Mary Stuart should be blocked, either by open opposition, or by ensuring that she was neutralised by marriage elsewhere.[31] To this end Cecil had pursued a subtle and disingenuous strategy; sometimes encouraging Scottish opponents of Mary in the belief that he was a staunch supporter; but at other times distancing himself from them when he considered it possible that other less confrontational ways might be found to neutralise Mary through, for instance, marriage to an English peer. His attitude provoked frustration and suspicion among Mary's enemies including Archibald Campbell, the 5th earl of Argyll.

A leader of the revolution against the French interest at the Scottish court, Argyll had become increasingly anxious to make friends with the English government in whatever way he could, as the prospect of the young Mary Stuart's imminent return to Scotland from France as rightful sovereign loomed.[32] As early as February 1560 he approached Cecil, offering to employ his forces in a campaign 'to reduce the north parts of Ireland to the perfect obedience of England'.[33] Cecil was encouraging, and in the following summer a perfect opportunity was presented to Argyll when he received a secret communication from Shane making a formal proposal of marriage to the earl's sister. Shane's motive was doubtless to rise above his unhappy alliance with the MacDonnells by relating himself to one of the most powerful mainland Scottish families. And his initiative indicates that he certainly believed Argyll was open to such a prospect. But the effort produced a wholly different effect. Argyll forwarded Shane's letters directly to Whitehall as a token of his goodwill and of his willingness to be of service to the English in the matter in whatever way they thought appropriate. Cecil proceeded on this basis to negotiate a secret alliance against Shane in which Argyll undertook to secure the defection of the MacDonnells from O'Neill and their pledge to support the crown in return for the recognition of their settlements in Antrim. An alliance between Argyll, the MacDonnells and Shane's Irish enemies, preparatory to a full-scale assault, was then cemented when the earl agreed to the marriage of his stepmother, Catherine MacLean, to Calvagh O'Donnell, lord of Tír Conaill.[34]

But further progress in these developing relationships was inhibited by the hostile attitude of the Irish governor, Sussex, who continued to argue that Argyll's motives in regard to Ulster were far from selfless. His real intention, Sussex insisted, was that of establishing a satellite MacDonnell lordship in the province under his direct authority. And this was to be firmly resisted. Despite the peace with Scotland, Sussex continued to insist throughout the early years of Elizabeth's reign that the expulsion of the Scots from Ulster was essential to the province's future stability. As invaders and suppliers of mercenary troops to all disaffected interests in Ulster, they had contributed almost as much as O'Neill to the region's continuing troubles and had provided, of course, the central means by which O'Neill and his Geraldine allies had conducted the politics of continuing aggression. Grudgingly, as his own military and diplomatic efforts failed, Sussex was persuaded by Cecil to relent and to open negotiations with Argyll as part of the alliance against O'Neill he was constructing at the beginning of 1561.[35] But by then Shane had become aware of the forces gathering against him, and he dissolved the threat by his seizure of Calvagh and his Scottish wife in May 1561.[36]

But even after this debâcle Cecil continued to work for alliance with Argyll that would enable him to use MacDonnells against Shane and gain a separate foothold in Gaelic Ulster. Thus late in

1561, even as arrangements for Shane's visit were being finalised, Cecil was writing to Sussex instructing him once again to open negotiations with James MacDonnell on the basis of his dealings with Argyll. And early in 1562, when Shane's mission to court was already well under way, Argyll wrote to Cecil urging him to negotiate the toughest possible terms with Shane, including the release of his captured step-mother, and renewing his promise to place all his forces at Cecil's disposal should another attempt on Shane be contemplated in the future.[37]

In these circumstances, the attractions of sustaining an uncompromising attitude toward Shane and his suits, at least in the short term, must have appeared to Secretary Cecil to be considerable. But they were richly enhanced by the even more immediate factors from which the pressures of court politics could not be excluded. 'To say that Elizabeth's council was not dominated by faction is one thing,' the historian Norman Jones has wisely observed, 'to argue that there was none is quite another.'[38] Factional impulses arising from the elaborate patronage and clientage networks of the Elizabethan political elite may have been dormant or constrained, but they were perfectly capable of being galvanised on particular occasions, most notably when issues normally peripheral to the business of the court moved to its centre, presenting an urgent challenge and also an immediate opportunity. Such was the case with Ireland.

It has been seen already how Sussex's broad reformist plans for Ireland were warped and narrowed through his perception of the infectious role of Irish factions, now the same process of distortion began to apply in Cecil's case, and from precisely the same source: his concern for the intrigues and stratagems of Gerald, the earl of Kildare. For Cecil the challenge posed to English government by the machinations of Kildare was by no means remote. Although Kildare's rehabilitation under Queen Mary had seemed complete, he had found himself cut off from the innermost circles of Elizabeth's court, where his principal rival, Thomas Butler, the 10th earl of Ormond, enjoyed a special relationship with the queen. Thus frustrated, he became the natural ally of that other much-mistrusted figure, himself the son of an attainted rebel, whose personal influence with Elizabeth, though uncertain, boded fair in the early 1560s to exceed all others: Lord Robert Dudley. For Dudley, Kildare's vast influence in Ireland promised rich sources of patronage and political intelligence, and in return Dudley was more than pleased to offer himself as a furtherer of Kildare and the interests of those, in particular Shane, whom he befriended.[39]

Friendship with Dudley, at this crucial juncture in the favourite's political ascent, inevitably aroused the suspicion of Secretary Cecil, who as the principal contender for Elizabeth's ear had most to fear from the favourite's ambition. By the time of Shane's arrival at Whitehall, the queen's secretary and the royal favourite had been locked in an intense struggle for over a year, and the outcome was still uncertain. For though Elizabeth had drawn back from offering the ultimate prize of marriage, she continued to indicate that Lord Robert was still her favourite. In this context, Sussex's analysis of faction in Ireland and its subversive effects acquired a greater relevance and urgency within the circle of Cecil and his supporters than it might otherwise have had. The nexus of English court politics and Irish provincial politics in the early 1560s thus resided in the mesh of interlocking factions. And at this crucial time, Shane was at the centre of the mesh.[40]

In overtly opposing Shane, and siding with Sussex, Cecil was motivated not only hostility to Dudley or loyalty to the beleaguered viceroy, but also by the conviction that he himself had found a way of solving the crown's troubles in Ulster, by integrating them into his own larger ambitions of constructing a broad British policy to safeguard the Protestant succession.[41] Thus Cecil calculatedly presided over the dilatory negotiations with Shane from February to April 1562, supporting Sussex's preconditions and then adding the final demands relating to the young Dungannon at the close, until Shane bolted, made his escape from Whitehall, and prepared for war.

And so the last chance to settle with O'Neill and stabilise the politics of Ulster within its own bounds was lost in the welter of national and international perspectives in which it had become embroiled. For Cecil and Sussex this was a successful result. But even as they triumphed, plans for an Anglo-Scottish alliance in Ulster dissolved as Argyll broke off communications with Whitehall and began to seek a new alliance with O'Neill. In the meantime, Dudley, frustrated with his Irish adventure, moved to find other means to outdo his rival, while a vengeful Kildare laboured to sabotage Sussex's campaign plans. An imperfect peace had been discarded in favour of an unwinnable war.

CHAPTER 5

Appeasement and Drift, 1562–5

Preparations for the war now made inevitable by the collapse of negotiations at court were begun by Shane immediately on his return to Ulster. He had, in fact, reason enough to hasten home, for in his absence many of the territories over which he claimed lordship had begun to assert their independence, with the support of the Dublin government. Turlough Luineach may have killed young Dungannon at Shane's prompting in April, but he had had himself proclaimed the O'Neill just days before Shane's return to Ulster in June. His effort soon collapsed, but it was nevertheless a sign of the disintegration of Shane's authority during his long detention in England. The English in Ulster had also played some part. The garrison at Armagh continued to extract supplies by force from the surrounding country, while Bagenal and Brereton had actually raided O'Neill's home territory, rustling large numbers of cattle ostensibly in reprisal for Shane's earlier raids on the Pale.[1]

Shane's return changed all this. In a systematic tour of the province, he made an example of Maguire, the chief who had been Sussex's closest ally, wasting his lordship and compelling the chieftain to go into hiding. Next he invaded Tír Conaill, spoiling the country of upwards of 30,000 head of cattle. After this he had little difficulty in securing the submission of O'Reilly and MacMahon, and he resumed his pressure on Dublin by resuming night raids on the garrison at Armagh and on the border villages of the Pale. Thus Shane made clear his rejection of the terms that had been forced on him in England, proclaiming before an assembly of the O'Neills 'that he went not into England to keep but to win'.[2]

This, of course, was what Sussex and Cecil had wanted. Even before Sussex's return, his caretaker, Lord Justice Fitzwilliam, had already begun the effort to persuade Elizabeth to make war, and immediately on his arrival in Dublin Sussex himself reiterated this view, fuelled by reports of Shane's latest outrages, that only the complete destruction of Shane would bring peace to Ulster. As ever, the viceroy's case was compelling on paper. Shane's ambitions toward provincial domination were now clear, and if nothing was done to withstand him, the loss of all those whose loyalty to the crown had remained steadfast under the most terrible of conditions was certain. But conversely, there were signs, even from within his own lordship, and most notably from Turlough Luineach, that renewed war against Shane would attract much internal support. And, most important of all, the MacDonnells were pledged to serve against him. This, then, was the moment to strike decisively at Shane in an action that would at once destroy the most dangerous power in Ireland and confirm the loyalties and affections of all the other Ulster dynasties. There was a certain ambiguity in Sussex's propaganda: if the allegiance of the Ulster lords was so heartfelt, why was it also so fragile? But at the time such tensions passed unnoticed amidst the urgency with which Sussex pressed his case.[3]

The inherent difficulty of this position only began to become apparent when the war strategy itself became enmeshed in the workings of that malign machine against which both Sussex and Cecil had erected their anti-Shane stance in the first place – the politics of faction. Almost immediately after his departure from court, the victory which Sussex believed he had secured over Dudley and his Geraldine friends began to dissolve. In the autumn of 1562 the endurance of Elizabeth's favour toward Dudley was marked by her unexpected assent to his ambitious scheme to revive England's interest in France by dispatching an expeditionary force in support of the French Protestants at Le Havre. Then in October Elizabeth was struck down by smallpox, and *in extremis* her dependence upon Dudley became even more pronounced. Nursed by Dudley's sister, Lady Mary Sidney, Elizabeth resumed her earlier favour to Dudley and distanced herself from his enemies, including Secretary Cecil; it was even rumoured that she had commanded that, in the event of her death, Dudley be made 'Lord Protector'. Amidst this crisis Sussex's campaign for another Irish war collapsed. Dudley, of course, was hostile. And Elizabeth herself, having committed to an adventure in France, was reluctant to stretch her resources by opening a second theatre in Ireland. Cecil did his best to sustain the queen's earlier resolution, but being himself now in temporary eclipse, even he lacked the influence to hold Elizabeth to a policy toward which she was no longer personally well disposed.[4] It was then that Shane (who seems to have been remarkably well informed of developments at court) sent an ambassador to Whitehall bearing letters and gifts to Dudley, Cecil and to Elizabeth, professing loyalty, renewing his suit for recognition and detailing the wrongs perpetrated against his lands and people during his absence. Elizabeth responded to Shane's diplomatic initiative by prevaricating: no decision could be made without consulting with Sussex. But by the time the matter was referred to Dublin at the beginning of 1563 the viceroy's resistance was already broken.[5]

The forces which had reduced Sussex to this condition operated principally in Ireland. But behind them also could be discerned the malign influence of the Dudley faction. As early as 1561, as part of his campaign to make friends in Ireland, the favourite had been influential in gaining an audience at court for a group of law students who presented a list of grievances against the conduct of Sussex's army in the Pale, and also in securing the

establishment of a commission of inquiry to test the veracity of
such complaints headed by a client of his own, Sir Nicholas
Arnold. Appointed early in 1562, Arnold had at first moved slowly,
but as Cecil's and Sussex's credit waned he grew more assertive,
until at length he fully endorsed the substance of the charges against
the army and recommended that a full audit of the captains'
accounts be undertaken before the next full pay was made. The
captains refused to present accounts, and in the midst of this intra-
administrative conflict the country revolted, refusing to grant
supplies and resisting attempts to billet the soldiers.[6] Thus in the
second half of 1562, as Sussex attempted to revive his war effort,
he found himself starved both of pay and basic supplies. Desperate,
he resorted to Irish mercenaries whose service was cheaper than
official troops but quite undependable. These were Sussex's circumstances when Shane seized the initiative by raids on the Pale and an
attack on the English garrison at Armagh. Compelled to react,
Sussex began his third campaign against Shane; and all the things
he had feared rapidly came to pass. Cecil failed to produce even the
small reinforcements and extra munitions he had promised, and
the Pale resisted, yielding up only a small portion of the supplies
requisitioned. The Irish kerne failed to appear, and Kildare, the
man who had promised to supply them, mysteriously fell sick.[7]

The doomed campaign of 1563 thus took its course. Sussex
made some raids into O'Neill territory, seizing cattle and burning
corn, but found no sign of Shane.[8] He tried again to assassinate
him (a clear sign of desperation) by sending 'one Smith' to poison
him with tampered wine.[9] This too failed, leaving Shane with no
more than a hangover and perfect grounds for his refusal to come
to the governor until a final peace had been concluded. By then, in
any case, the ramshackle coalition Sussex had cobbled together had
begun to come apart as in their own different ways the Ulster lords,
the Palesmen and the English soldiers themselves gradually

defected from the enterprise.[10] It was the familiar pattern, but this time one additional element was decisive. Even before Sussex began, Elizabeth, under Dudley's urgings, had granted permission for Sir Thomas Cusack, the former lord chancellor under St Leger and frequent negotiator with O'Neill, to present his views on the best way of dealing with Shane.

Cusack's advice was unequivocal. Following the debâcle in 1562 and Sussex's present fiasco, it was vital that a permanent settlement be reached with Shane not by force but by diplomacy. Elizabeth agreed, and in July she directed Sussex to cease operations forthwith and to co-operate with Cusack in arranging negotiations.[11] In a personal communication she made clear also that she would brook no resistance, and that Sussex's public humiliation was a price she was willing to pay.[12] Ruin: Sussex capitulated and appears to have suffered a complete nervous collapse that effectively ended his viceroyalty.[13]

The treaty negotiated by Cusack with Shane at Drumcree in September 1563 granted O'Neill almost everything he had sought at court and by implication a good deal more.[14] All previous treaties between Shane and the crown were superseded, and the humiliating conditions wrung from him in April 1562 were now formally extinguished. Acknowledging Shane as 'the Lord O'Neill', a title used in the past to signify close and friendly relations with the crown, the treaty promised that Shane would proceed to assume the earldom once the Dungannon title had been extinguished by statute (the only method, Cusack had cleverly insisted, by which Shane's new title could be made free from challenge). Shane's claim to overlordship in Ulster was recognised in terms echoing those of 1542: he was to have 'the leading and service of so many lords and captains as shall be proved to have of ancient custom appertained to such as . . . held the place of O'Neill.'[15] And the implications of this concession were explicitly endorsed in a clause

concerning Shane's outstanding disputes with O'Reilly and
Maguire which effectively granted Shane's *prima facie* case. Shane's
suit to become a commissioner to hear causes in Ulster was agreed
to. His demand for the evacuation of the garrison from Armagh
and the restoration of ecclesiastical jurisdiction there was accepted.
His requirement that Smith, the poisoner, should be brought to
trial was agreed to. And his related request to be allowed to seek
assurances for his safety before coming to the viceroy was granted.
Even his suit to have an English noblewoman found who might
become his wife was received with the assurance that the queen
herself would join in the search.[16]

Cusack and Arnold were confident that the concessions granted
at Drumcree were sufficient to compensate for the mistrust which
had made Shane so dangerous in the past. And Shane himself gave
every indication that he was sincere in his desire to reach a final
settlement. Yet for all its apparent generosity, the treaty constituted no more than a pious declaration of intent that required
confirmation in the form of concrete political action before its
promised benefits could be realised. And even the earliest attempts
to honour its terms revealed just how difficult the process was to
prove in practice. The first of these unexpectedly difficult issues
concerned the concession made to Shane that he need not answer
the viceroy's summons without sureties for his safety. At the time
it was granted, given Sussex's several attempts to kill O'Neill by
stealth, the privilege seemed no more than an indication of the
government's good faith. But at the beginning of 1564, after Sussex
had been sequestered and replaced as governor by Nicholas Arnold,
the provision seemed both unnecessary and discreditable, granting
O'Neill the status not of a subject, but of independent power who
could deal with the Irish sovereign as equal. This was, of course,
unacceptable; and recognising it as such, Elizabeth herself refused
to sanction it, striking it out from the later drafts of the treaty

which had been drawn up for her ratification. Angered by this unilateral alteration, and suspecting that it could be used as a means by which the whole treaty could be set aside, Shane at first insisted on retaining the original article, until Cusack at last persuaded him of the valid constitutional grounds on which Elizabeth had made her stand and, reluctantly, Shane let the matter drop.[17]

This was an unfortunate misunderstanding. But the mistrust engendered by the delay in ratification was further developed by the crown's default in regard to two unrelated and relatively minor matters. One was the failure to make any effort at all to further Shane's quest for an English wife – a desire which appears to have been greeted with a mixture of horror and ridicule at court. But a more serious matter was the failure to apprehend Smith and have him brought to trial. These evasions were sources of insult and irritation. But by the middle of 1564, after almost a year in which he had on his part honoured the peace, Shane had reason to be concerned at the government's failure to honour the central promise of Drumcree, that was the commitment to expunge the Dungannon title and confer the earldom on Shane by statute.[18]

Whatever about the crown's disingenuousness in regard to Smith and a well-born English wife, it seems clear that a genuine desire existed in both Dublin and Whitehall for the summoning of an Irish parliament which would enact legislation on a whole range of matters – not least religious and ecclesiastical reform – other than the settlement of Ulster. But the calling of parliament also raised a whole set of thorny political issues both in Ireland and at court which were quite independent of the problem of O'Neill. In Ireland, intensifying conflict between the earls of Ormond and Desmond, full-scale rebellion in the midlands and the deepening hostility of the English-Irish community of the Pale toward the English garrison augured ill for any grand programme of legislative reform. Caution counselled delay. But the question of an Irish parliament also raised problems of an equally acute if rather different kind at court. Given the immense significance of calling an Irish parliament, it was clear that the task of its management could not be delegated to the caretaker office of lord justice which Sir Nicholas Arnold now held. The options before Elizabeth were, therefore, either to reinstall Sussex, to elevate Arnold (a proposal which he himself vigorously canvassed) or to find someone else who was acceptable at court, and who would be held in sufficient respect by all sides in Ireland to enable him to conduct the affairs of parliament with due authority. The question, then, of the Irish parliament and of Shane's title thus became integral to the intensive intrigues of court politics as rival interests led by Cecil and Dudley competed to exercise a dominant influence over the appointment of an Irish viceroy. Characteristically, Elizabeth prevaricated, and the decision on the timing of parliament was again and again deferred.[19]

This delay was a source of anxiety and frustration to Shane of a far greater magnitude than any of his other disappointments with the treaty. For the failure to settle his title by statute was the clearest indication that, for all his formidable power in Ulster, he still lacked the ability to convince the government of the vital importance of pacifying Ulster by settling the status of O'Neill. And although he was regularly assured by Dublin of its intention to resolve his position by statute, every day's delay increased the fear that Dungannon's case was not altogether lost, or that the crown might not revive the earldom at all.

This long stalemate compelled Shane to take action in the summer of 1564. Petitioning to be allowed to do some service to demonstrate his loyalty, Shane proposed a full-scale assault on the MacDonnells and, having first consulted with Dudley and Cecil, secured permission from Arnold to proceed with the design. His own object in mounting this new war was clear. Given the threat to his position in Ulster arising out of the government's failure to complete the provisions of Drumcree, it was imperative that he once again mobilise his supporters, and discourage his enemies by another demonstration of his formidable strength. But he remained anxious to tie Dublin to his enterprise, requesting to have the English garrison at Carrickfergus placed at his disposal. On this point Arnold demurred, but he did instruct William Piers, the constable there, to offer whatever supplies he could. This was enough for Shane, who now proceeded on his campaign on the assumption that whatever benefits accrued to him as O'Neill from victory over the Scots would not weaken his case with the English government to be created earl of Tyrone.[20]

To begin with, success evaded him. Abandoning his normal methods of indirect intrigue and guerrilla war, Shane challenged the MacDonnells to do battle on the banks of the Bann. They met the challenge, forcing Shane's army back across the river and destroying the fort he had constructed to mount the operation. This was bad, but not catastrophic. For neither Shane nor the Scots were disposed to bring the conflict to a final conclusion. Thus a truce was briskly agreed. But within Ulster the reverberations of the reverse, coupled with the need to do something to placate the Scots, obliged Shane to turn toward another operation, one which was not at all sanctioned by the English government, against his great provincial rival in Tír Conaill.[21]

Even before he moved against the Scots in the middle of 1564, Shane had taken steps to reaffirm his authority in Tír Conaill by securing the surrender of Lifford Castle and the promise of a large ransom as the price for the release of Calvagh O'Donnell. Once free, Calvagh resorted first to Dublin and then to Whitehall, where throughout late 1564 he recounted (with little effect) the horrible suffering he had endured at the hands of the bestial O'Neill. In the meantime, however, no ransom was paid from Tír Conaill; so in the early summer Shane, taking advantage of the internal strife among the sons and nephews of O'Donnell, invaded and devastated the country, seizing hundreds of thousands of cattle and in a violent spree, equalled only by his own civil war in the 1550s, killing, according to reports, thousands of the lordship's meagre population.[22]

Thus satisfied, Shane had turned in the summer to face the MacDonnells; but now following his disappointment against them, he felt obliged in the autumn to return again to Tír Conaill in order to restore his authority, replenish resources, and assure his soldiers that there was still plenty of booty to be had by remaining in his service. Thus he settled permanent garrisons in the principal castles of Tír Conaill and established a puppet regime of his own there by his recognition of Hugh Dubh O'Donnell, Calvagh's brother, in opposition to the chief and his sons. This virtual occupation of Tír Conaill was noted with some concern in Whitehall, where the exiled Calvagh again reported terrifying details of the state of affairs in his lordship.[23] But in Dublin, where Arnold and Cusack were still committed to Drumcree, reaction to these developments was more complacent. Responding to criticism from court concerning his failure to restrain Shane, Arnold offered two levels of justification. Until he had satisfied himself about the security of Tír Conaill, Arnold argued, there was no chance that Shane would commit himself wholly against the Scots, which was the shared objective of Dublin and Whitehall. But more fundamentally he reasoned that Shane's occupation of Tír Conaill was necessarily a temporary and possibly a fatal adventure: in order to be sure of Tír Conaill, Shane would have to colonise it with his own people, a strategy which, given the relative poverty of the place, he would never attempt. But the alternative military rule he was now imposing was equally defective, for the great oppressions he habitually visited on occupied territories would simply breed more enemies for his regime in the future. His attempt to dominate a divided Tír Conaill would eventually result in its unification.[24] All of this was shrewd, but it was also contradictory. For while Arnold was speculating happily about Shane's eventual nemesis, he was also encouraging, in his support for the war against the Scots, the very strategy which might enable Shane to escape it. In fact this justification of inaction was just another way of surrendering the initiative to Shane; and again, as so often in the past, Shane seized whatever initiative became available to him.

The desired opportunity was once more presented by the Scots. Early in 1565 James MacDonnell returned to Ireland with a major force and, with the aid of the MacDonnells settled in Clandeboy, began a major push southward through County Down. The attack enabled Shane to pose as the defender of the native Irish against the Scots, and so with the support of the local dynasties he began a second major assault on the MacDonnells. This was a carefully considered operation. First Shane cut off the Scottish raiding parties in Down, leaving them to the mercy of the local families. Then, by cutting passes, he marched unexpectedly into the Glens and the Route and besieged the MacDonnell fortress at Red Bay. Having destroyed it, and wasted the surrounding territory, he moved next to the second major MacDonnell emplacement, Sorley Boy MacDonnell's fortress at Ballycastle. The Scots appeared in force to defend it, and close to the castle in the valley of Glentaisie, battle was joined on 2 May 1565.[25]

It was a bloody affair with heavy losses on both sides, but at close of the day it was clear that Shane had won. More than 600 Scots were killed and more were taken prisoner, including James MacDonnell and his brother Sorley Boy. Shane lost no time in capitalising on his triumph, seizing and destroying the MacDonnells' castles along the coast, and capturing Dunluce Castle by threatening to kill Sorley Boy right in front of it. But he went further. Rejecting all offers of

ransom, including the surrender of James MacDonnell's lands in
Scotland, he began colonising the Glens and the Route, settling his
own people there in large numbers and establishing garrisons to
protect them. He remained east of the Bann throughout the summer
of 1565, overseeing the new settlement and renegotiating terms
with the lesser native families of Clandeboy. The first sixteenth-
century plantation of Ulster had begun.[26]

The ominous implications of Shane's new Ulster initiative
were soon made clear. Over the closing months of 1565 he sought
to secure his gains by opportunist expansionism. He invaded East
Breifne [Cavan], supporting Cahir O'Reilly in his claims against
the new chieftain Hugh (or Aodh Connallach), thus neutralising
Breifne as a potential enemy. Late in the year he led an expedition
into Connacht, spoiling O'Rourke of more than 4,000 cattle, quarter-
ing his troops and declaring his intention to revive the ancient
tribute which he claimed O'Rourke and his neighbours in north
Connacht had traditionally owed the O'Neills. More seriously still,
Shane moved against the English in Ulster, expelling the garrisons
from Dundrum and from Newry. But most seriously of all, he
reopened communications with the earl of Argyll, now out of favour
at the court in Edinburgh, in another effort to find an alliance with
a Scottish interest superior to the MacDonnells.[27]

All of this was fatal to the policy of appeasement. For it
was clear now that, just as Shane had transcended the abortive
negotiations of 1562, he had also gone beyond the stalled treaty of
Drumcree and was now seeking an even higher level to convince
the crown of the necessity of granting him recognition. The
position he now adopted as an independent and potentially hostile
force with interests spreading west, south and eastward toward
Scotland put him well beyond even the most generous recognition
promised by Drumcree, and was disastrous for those who claimed
that it would contain him. Thus Dean Donnelly's hopes to be

elevated to the see of Armagh were dashed; Thomas Cusack's imminent reappointment as lord chancellor was rescinded; and Arnold, who had expected promotion to the viceroyalty as lord deputy, was given notice of recall.[28] But for the bigger players in the diplomatic game of courting Shane, for Kildare and Dudley, stark lessons were learned. For Shane had now shown that he could never be drawn to play the subordinate role in their factional designs for which they were preparing him. And since he would not conform, he must be destroyed.

Thus in the spring of 1565 Dudley (now earl of Leicester) and Kildare abruptly changed their minds and, abandoning Arnold, began to promote Leicester's brother-in-law, Sir Henry Sidney, as Sussex's replacement in the Irish office. A man who was at once popular in Ireland, especially in the Pale, and, following his service as treasurer-at-war, respected by the garrison there, Sidney would inspire none of the rancour which Sussex and Arnold had in their different ways provoked. As a figure, moreover, who had both negotiated with and campaigned against Shane in the past, he was more suited than any to determine how Shane was to be handled. On this issue Leicester and Sidney had no doubt: Shane was to be brought down by war. But the problem was, oddly enough, to persuade the queen to accept this view. For the same set of developments which had converted former appeasers to the necessity of war had also convinced Elizabeth of the need to proceed with caution. Despite all urgings, she still refused to commit herself. And, ironically, just as the campaign to rescue Shane in 1562 had originally been fought at court, it was requisite that the campaign to destroy him must first take place there also.

CHAPTER 6

War, 1566–7

If Sidney, Leicester and Kildare had any sense of the irony of their position, they never showed it, but worked vigorously through the autumn of 1565 to convince Elizabeth to sanction all out war. Yet through successive drafts of Sidney's instructions, Elizabeth refused to give a decision, and he arrived in Ireland early in 1566 with his standing already somewhat diminished in the queen's eye, and without any stronger authority than an oracular directive to the effect that if Shane should prove to be wholly intractable, Sidney should 'let him remain as he doth to receive that which he shall deserve at our hands.'[1]

Indecision thus paralysed the first months of Sidney's administration, and it was only at the close of March that Secretary Cecil who, having been cool toward Sidney over the previous year, now came forward with a proposal of his own. The question as to what policy to adopt against Shane, Cecil suggested, should be referred to the judgement of an independent observer, the vice-chamberlain of the royal household, Sir Francis Knollys. A close confidant of Elizabeth, and a courtier with a long record of distinguished service, Knollys was acknowledged by all to be above the sordid intrigues of faction. But as a committed Protestant with a strong desire to further true Reformation, he had some sympathy for Leicester, who, for less disinterested motives, was an equally enthusiastic promoter of Protestant policies and personnel. Thus the vice-chamberlain was accepted as an impartial referee by all. The instructions drafted for him were, accordingly, broad and vaguely cast. There is some evidence that Elizabeth herself had hoped for a recommendation from Knollys which would confirm her own predilection for inaction. But in the event, following his independent review of the state of Ulster and the condition of the English garrison, and his extensive consultations within the Dublin administration, Knollys submitted an unequivocal report confirming the case for war and approving Sidney's preparations for the coming campaign.[2]

Knollys' mission thus accomplished everything for which Sidney and Leicester had hoped, and attached into the bargain some credit to Cecil, whose idea it had been in the first place. Yet all of this had been achieved only at the cost of considerable waste of time. At the outset Sidney had hoped to begin his campaign as early as March, but Knollys did not complete his report until mid-June. Only then did the cumbersome Tudor logistical machine begin to turn, and even then the delays were worse than usual. Sidney was promised troops and supplies for July, but they were finally dispatched to Ireland only at the beginning of September, and it was only at the end of the month that Sidney had gathered sufficient force to commence his journey north. Having lost three-quarters of his first year in office in strategic and logistical wrangles, Sidney was at length forced to begin operations with a winter campaign.[3]

In the meantime Shane had been making his own preparations for the coming conflict. In the summer he had campaigned in the west, again attacking Maguire and strengthening his hold in Tír Conaill by seizing more castles. He then invaded O'Reilly and wasted his country. More sinisterly, he resumed his diplomatic efforts on an even more ambitious scale than before, entering into a Byzantine intrigue with Argyll in which he seems to have offered to profess allegiance to Queen Mary of Scotland or otherwise, according to whatever Argyll himself considered appropriate.[4] More ambitiously still, he addressed Charles IX of France and his brother the Cardinal of Lorraine, promising fealty to the French crown should the king choose to invade Ireland.[5] These gambits in Scotland and France were purely speculative: some of the correspondence in regard to the former was forged, some in regard to the latter was never received. There are grounds for suspicion that in both cases the letters were designed for interception by English intelligence agents (which is precisely what happened) to serve as a means of showing just how serious Shane was in preparing for the imminent war. But it is worth noting that, at the time of their dispatch, Shane was as yet under no immediate threat from the viceroy still in the throes of his organisational travails, but had already begun the diplomatic preparation for a long war.

That he had accepted the inevitability of war is evident also in his conduct once the Knollys commission had been completed. In late summer he resumed his terror campaign in the Pale, burning towns all along the border, and laying siege to Drogheda for several weeks. He began internal preparations also, evacuating Dungannon and Benburb and divesting Armagh of its treasure and plate. Thus when Sidney at last moved into Ulster, there was nothing of substance for him to attack or destroy. So he journeyed north-westwards, traversing Tír Eoghain, but never encountering the enemy. On one occasion Shane showed himself from afar with a force of more than 2,000 men, but then disappeared. Sidney then left Tír Eoghain without incident or success and crossed the Foyle, where he reconnoitred with Edmund Randolph, the 'colonel' of the garrison which had been established by Sidney at the old ruined monastery of Derry.[6]

The fort at Derry had been envisaged as a key element in Sidney's war strategy, being designed to serve as the second arm of a pincer-movement by which Shane, having been squeezed out of the south of Tír Eoghain, would find himself trapped in the north. But having failed to encounter Shane, and finding that supplies in Tír Conaill were insufficient to allow a march back through mid-Ulster, Sidney changed plans and moved south toward Sligo and Roscommon, leaving Randolph to face the winter alone. It was then that Shane emerged to challenge Derry. Battle ensued, and though the English sources report (doubtfully) that Shane lost heavily and the garrison only one man, that loss – Colonel Randolph himself – was crucial. Thereafter, serving little purpose other than sustaining its own survival by feeding off an increasingly hostile hinterland, the garrison began to disintegrate, and at length destroyed itself through an explosion of its own gunpowder in April 1567.[7]

Meanwhile Sidney had sought to sustain the morale of his troops and his Ulster allies by launching a surprise raid on Tír Eoghain in the depths of winter. In his memoirs, written almost twenty years later, he was to make much of the achievement. Claiming to have been the first to attempt such a winter adventure (St Leger, in fact, had conducted a far more successful winter-time raid against Conn Bacach in 1540–1), he boasted to have come within an ace of capturing Shane amidst his Christmas festivities, but Shane 'ran away, and so I shortened his Christmas and made an end of my own with abundance of his good provisions'.[8] This was not, however, how Sidney expressed himself at the time. Then, maddened by criticism and obstruction at court, he was, like Sussex, pleading for recall and repeating the conviction that unless massive reinforcements were sent, Shane would triumph over everyone in the coming year. He had good grounds for such a view. During Sidney's absence in the west in the closing months of 1566 Shane had intensified his raids on the Pale, again threatening the walls of Drogheda. He showed how moved he was by Sidney's Yuletide

surprise by dispatching a letter to Dublin early in the new year,
offering peace, but only on the basis of the terms agreed with
Cusack at Drumcree.[9]

As the new campaign season drew near, however, Sidney, like
Sussex before him, became more positive. It now appeared that
Randolph and his futile Ulster journey had done Shane some
damage after all. His staunchest friends among the O'Cahans and
the O'Hanlons were reported to have become estranged from him;
O'Reilly had restored order in Breifne and had sworn to protect the
Pale; the MacDonnells had sworn vengeance against him; and
Hugh O'Donnell, his former ally, had deserted him immediately
upon the death of Calvagh O'Donnell and was now laying claim to
the lordship of Tír Conaill, 'so that O'Neill is, as it were, cooped in
Tyrone'. Such optimistic posturings were, as in the past, part of
the propaganda campaign required to persuade Elizabeth to release
more resources for another year's war, and they were inevitably
accompanied by repeated requests for one last commitment of
men and money.[10]

Propagandist purposes notwithstanding, there remained, however,
an essential element of truth in all these rumours about disaffection
surrounding Shane. Reported defections among his own followers
were, of course, either dubious or ephemeral; but they were sympto-
matic of a deeper weakness in Shane's political position. For the price
of his war, waged continually with only brief respites since his rise
to power in the early 1550s, had been extremely high. Economically,
losses through retaliation and the need to evacuate stores were
painful; but in political terms also, subordinate allies, such as O'Cahan
and O'Hanlon, found it increasingly difficult to maintain authority
over their own followers in the pursuit of the great O'Neill's permanent war. There was, then, as Sir Nicholas Arnold had cynically
noted, an intrinsic countervailing force to Shane's expansionism:
the more demands he made on his subjects to supply his ever-

increasing army, the more enemies he made among his own people and among those who feared they could be next. Such were the inherent fault-lines of the O'Neill lordship, and Shane, recognising them, had since his accession bent his career to find a way of transcending them. But given the alternating eagerness, obduracy and indolence of the crown, he had perforce been driven to sustain the O'Neill's belligerent address, steadily racking up the stakes even now to the point of inviting foreign intervention in order to secure his essentially provincial objectives.

Ever present, such weaknesses were not, however, any more obvious when Shane began the campaign season of 1567. Not surprisingly, he began in Tír Conaill, where he determined to punish his treacherous former ally, Hugh O'Donnell. Preliminary scoutings confirmed Hugh's weakness among the O'Donnells themselves. Thus in April he invaded with a force of 2,000 men to repeat the ravages of 1565. The new, much-mistrusted O'Donnell summoned the country to repel the invader. Nobody budged; and thus humiliated, Hugh withdrew to his own fastnessess.[11] Shane then settled his army at the great ford of Fearsat Suibhle (Farsetmore), a crossing-point traditionally favoured by the O'Neills for the transfer of booty and the supply of reinforcements – a clear sign that a prolonged occupation was about to begin. It was this realisation that suddenly changed Hugh O'Donnell's status in Tír Conaill. Former enemies such as the O'Dohertys and the MacSwiney chieftains of Fanad, Banagh and Doe flocked to him, and the dissident O'Donnells for once united behind him. Hugh seized the opportunity and made an unexpected appearance before the camp at Farsetmore. As he had with the Scots at the Bann, Shane underestimated the challenge and prepared for battle. But when his line broke, overwhelmed by the unanticipated strength of the O'Donnell alliance, there was nowhere left to retreat, for Hugh had timed the attack to coincide with the high-tide of the

Swilly. Thus forced into the river, the bulk of Shane's army perished; 600, the sources say, died in the field, 1,300 in the water. Shane himself escaped northwards with a tiny remnant; but among the dead at Farsetmore were his constable, the commander of his Scottish mercenaries, and Dubhaltach O'Donnelly, 'his own foster-brother and the person most dear to him in existence', the man who had killed Dungannon.[12]

This defeat, occurring at the very start of the campaign season, was the disaster Shane had often risked but long evaded; and his enemies now closed in. Art MacBaron, the illegitimate son of Dungannon, made a first appearance as a dangerous opponent; Turlough Luineach renewed his old rebellion; Sidney prepared to move north. But most seriously of all, the Scots reappeared on the Antrim coast in great force. Desperate, Shane vacillated. Later, it was to be reported in sources that he considered submitting totally to Sidney, coming to him with a halter around his neck. But in fact Shane elected for the traditional policy of negotiating with the Scots.[13]

With the benefit of hindsight, his decision may be seen to have been fatally misguided: the slaughter at Glentaisie had earned him the Scots' implacable enmity. But from the perspective of June 1567, Shane's action was not altogether reckless. Vengeance had a short half-life in sixteenth-century Irish politics, and there were grounds enough for Shane to hope that a new accommodation could be reached. He had already made peace with some of the MacDonnells, employing their services in his operations in 1566. He still held Sorley Boy as a hostage, though reports had it that by now Sorley was a willing companion, and Alexander Óg, the new chieftain, had, despite his promises to Sidney, as yet refrained from attacking Shane.[14]

By now, however, the Scots had considerations other than the traditional strategies of dynastic politics in mind. From the beginning of his service Sidney had been pressing for the recognition of a permanent MacDonnell settlement in Ulster both as a buffer against O'Neill and as a barrier to further the Scots' invasions. Elizabeth rejected the idea as an offence to conventional international dynastic practices. But Sidney persisted, enlisting Sir Francis Knollys as a supporter, and securing permission to pursue an intrigue to convince the Scots that such a deal might be in the offing.[15] There is no reason to assume that such a design, elaborated through the medium of William Piers at Carrickfergus, should easily have duped the Scots. But two contrasting aspects of Shane's condition may independently have shaped their decision. One was their perception of his present weakness, a vulnerability which he had not experienced since the crises of the early 1550s; but the other, paradoxically, was their recognition of his terrifying potential strength, their awareness that, if Shane should survive this current emergency, he would attempt even more ambitious schemes, including the resettlement of the whole of Ulster and the total exclusion of the Scots in order to obtain the safe foundation of his lordship. Thus when he came to Cushendun on the 31 May, there was no feasting and no drunken frenzy. Talks were held over two days in carefully controlled conditions, negotiations between both sides taking place in an open field away from their respective forces and with only five advisers apiece. And when on the 2 June Shane failed to convince the Scots that they could after all live with him in Ireland, 'instead of sweet words, [they] cut his throat with a scian, and the five that was with him went not back to tell no tales.'[16]

No tales were told right then: the story of murder at the feast appeared only two years later, in the preamble to the act declaring Shane's treason and attainder for all of the reasons outlined in chapter 1. Instead, in the immediate aftermath of the killing – with the remnants of his army dispersed, Shane was buried quietly in a ruined monastery, with an old kerne's shirt as a winding-sheet. It was only four days later that Piers arrived from Carrickfergus, had the body exhumed, decapitated, and the head, 'pickled in a pipkin' sent to be displayed on a pole in Dublin Castle.[17] Afterwards everyone sought to claim a share in the event: Sidney, Piers, Turlough Luineach and, of course, the Scots. No doubt each played a part. But the circumstances of his killing and the strange delay in handing over his body suggest that, like so much in his life, Shane's death was not preordained, but the result of immediate calculation, expediency, and chance.

Conclusion

'In international affairs,' A. J. P. Taylor once quipped, 'there was nothing wrong with Hitler, except that he was a German.'[1] Historical parallels are anachronistic, yet it can similarly be said that in the world of sixteenth-century Irish politics there was nothing particularly vicious about Shane O'Neill, except that he was the O'Neill. Having been born into the lordship in the midst of its last attempts to secure stability by means of diplomacy, he came of age at the point when those efforts had begun to disintegrate. In seeking his own survival, he contributed greatly to the reshaping of O'Neill and Ulster politics in the years following this breakdown, most markedly by the massive escalation of violence which occurred in the province after mid-century. In the civil war by which he established his ascendancy, in the assaults on his father and the baron of Dungannon in the later 1550s, in his plundering of Breifne and Fermanagh in the early 1560s and his devastation of Tír Conaill in 1564–5, Shane deployed a level of violence which was unprecedented both in its intensity and in its merciless involvement of non-combatants. In part this was a product of his own uncertain beginnings – the fact that at the outset he counted for little among the O'Neills. But it was also due to developments beyond Tír Eoghain – the decision of the MacDonnells after 1550 to settle in Ulster. The Scots presence transformed the province's politics. If Shane had not been the first to exploit them, someone else would have done so; and it is part of the irony of his career that having been the one with least to lose by attaching himself to the invaders, the damage they inflicted on him grew proportionately with the success they delivered.

There is no reason to suppose that Shane was unaware of the predicament into which his resort to violence had placed him, or that the banal nemesis of those who live by the sword, prescribed for him by moralising historians from his own day down to ours, had escaped his intelligence. His own career had, after all, been fraught with danger. He narrowly escaped death at Dungannon's hands in 1552, and in the midst of his successes in the later 1550s a chance encounter with Felim Rua O'Neill of the Fews almost spelled his end. One of Sussex's assassination attempts came close; and Sidney, perhaps, really did spoil his Christmas dinner. He almost drowned in the Bann in his first unsuccessful war against the Scots. These were the risks attendant on such a strategy in good times and in bad; and eventually the odds began to count against him at Farsetmore and at Cushendun.

To this clear appreciation of the extreme fragility of his position deriving from his dependence on the costly, treacherous and self-interested Scots may be attributed several of the bolder initiatives with which he has been credited. Thus the report that he was he first among the Gaelic lords to set about the arming and training of his own peasantry may have been, if true, less a bold and forward-looking innovation than a symptom of his desperation; and his willingness to hire English mercenaries at great expense, as reported by Thomas Phetyplace, a further indication of his intense desire to free himself from the unwanted consquences of his early rise to power.[2] Similarly his audacious attempt to colonise the Glens of Antrim with his own people can been seen as a further, radical way of liberating himself from the Scots.[3] Yet from the outset the principal means by which Shane had sought an escape from his dilemma was that chosen by every previous O'Neill who had pursued internal stability by establishing a firm and lasting alliance with a power greater in its potential than his or any other local or regional option – the English crown. From the time of his association with St Leger to the frustrating negotiations at court and the treaty agreed at Drumcree, Shane had been engaged in a persistent campaign to convince the crown that the O'Neill could indeed be fitted into a new English order; and the more his overtures failed, the more he was obliged to make his demands from an increasingly commanding position in order to persuade the crown that it must accept him.

Behind the government's inability to come to terms with Shane there lay not one reason but several. The English mistrusted Shane's ambition, abhorred the violence with which he pursued it; and they became increasingly concerned with the geopolitical implications of his ambivalent relations with Scotland. But beneath all this there lay deeper, largely implicit, conditions militating against any effective rapprochement. One was simply a structural and functional flaw that was inherent in the Tudor political regime as a whole: that is, its incapacity to generate coherent policy, to sustain it and to control its unintended consequences.[4] It was the failure to uphold the reform policies of the early 1540s and their interruption for short-term security measures that precipitated the crisis in Tír Eoghain in 1551, and it was the private operations of the agents of this security policy that discredited Dungannon and his pro-government side and enabled Shane to emerge as the defender of his people. Yet when Shane himself trod the road to Dublin, his own initiative became enmeshed in Sussex's larger commitment against the Geraldine faction in Ireland, and his mission to court failed amidst the intrigues of England's own elite factions. When the paralysis engendered there was relieved, largely by Shane's own actions, the new policy of appeasement was itself neutralised, in part by factional obstruction, but also by the sheer inability of the crown to activate its central instrument of political reform, parliament. Factional calculations in regard to the early 1560s in particular, and in regard to sixteenth-century Ireland in general remained of greater significance than has recently been argued. But underlying them, conditioning their operation and their intensity, was, as the matter of summoning parliament itself indicates, an even deeper defect that was essentially ideological in character.

Attempts to trace the roots of Elizabethan thinking about Ireland and the Irish to some vague Renaissance anthropology or some simple account of Calvinist theology have obscured far deeper, more pervasive and more readily demonstrable ideological impulses which were all the more potent precisely because they were not expressed in explicitly argumentative texts, but because they were embedded in the institutions, procedures and attendant quotidian documents of the English legal system. The principles of English common law, of land tenure, contract, rights of succession, and change by statute were so deeply cherished by those active in English governance and politics that they sustained, in a largely implicit and uncritical manner, the conviction that English culture could be revived and extended in Ireland through the application of the same legal principles and procedures and the reconstruction of the same administrative and judicial institutions which had apparently brought such remarkable stability to the English polity.[5] Now the potential exposure of their limitations and their ineffectuality outside of the most controlled circumstances in England itself opened what, in the words of a much later common-law judge, could be described as 'an appalling vista' against which the English common-law mind instinctively revolted. That revulsion was in good part heightened by an acute and practical awareness of the English constitutional tradition's actual historical fragility, as attested to by the breakdown of royal authority in the late fifteenth century, the prolonged dynastic crisis of the mid-sixteenth century, and most immediately the deepening uncertainty over the present queen's marriage intentions. In this context Shane's inadvertent revelation of the weakness of the common-law tradition in Ireland through his insistence on the legitimate status of the Gaelic dynasties and his demonstration – in the best legal manner – that recognition of this status had been granted in practice by the English crown down to his own time, constituted a profound challenge which had to be confronted and overcome.

But with all of these rigid and anxious English constitutional intricacies, Shane O'Neill could, understandably, have had little patience. As the events detailed in the chapters above have indicated, he had by diplomatic and military means done everything possible to attain recognition from the crown as the rightful heir to the earldom of Tyrone which would have enabled him to begin the process of a permanent settlement anew; until at length frustration and the awareness that his long dalliance with the English had weakened his standing in Ulster impelled him to attempt ever greater demonstrations of his power, always increasing the chances that his political imperatives would soon outrun his military resources. His actions in 1565 terminated a peace policy that had long been moribund. But having driven him to reach so far, the war policy of the crown, afflicted by the same political and organi-sational obstacles that had ruined the peace, could do no more than indirectly undermine Shane's efforts, and wait until the risks always attendant upon his strategy eventually confounded him. The exigent manner of his removal allowed, however, of no great clarification in English policy: Sidney remained imprisoned by faction; the Scots were betrayed. Two years later in 1569, in the act of attainder, Sidney would evolve a grand historical narrative designed to marginalise Shane, and suppress all the constitutional and historical embarrassments he had presented.[6] But it too would prove ineffective, paralysed by the same combination of political interests and constitutional scruples which had undermined the crown's dealings in Ulster over the previous decade.[7] And in the midst of the recurring cycles of intervention and inaction that had brought Shane down, two other O'Neills, one a much exaggerated 'enemy', the other a gravely misjudged 'friend' emerged to take his place.

Detail from a map by John Speed, *c.* 1600

Notes

Abbreviation: TNA, SP 60, 61, 62, 63 refers throughout to The [British] National Archives, State Papers Ireland, Henry VIII, Edward VI, Mary I, Elizabeth I respectively.

Chapter 1: *The Legend of Shane the Proud: A Myth and Its Uses*

1 For a hostile survey see Thomas Moore, 'Shane O'Neill and the English historians', in *Irish Monthly* XLV (1917), pp 113–30.

2 John Hooker, 'A chronicle of Ireland, 1547–86', in Raphael Holinshed (ed.), *Chronicles* (3 vols, London, 1587), III, p. 113; see also Edmund Campion, *Two Bokes of the Historie of Ireland*, A. F. Vossen (ed.), (Assen, 1963), pp 138–42.

3 For a concise summary of such ready judgements see J. A. Froude, *The History of England from the Fall of Wolsey to the Defeat of the Armada* (12 vols, London, 1856–70), VII, ch. 7; see also the comments of the normally judicious Robert Dunlop in his biographical sketch in the *Dictionary of National Biography*; see also R. J. McNeill's supposedly objective assessment in *Encyclopedia Britannica* (11th edn, London, 1911), XX, pp 108–9, and Richard Bagwell, *Ireland under the Tudors* (3 vols, London, 1885–90), II, pp 118–19.

4 The story was first made current in the long preamble to the 'Act for the attainder of Shane O'Neill', 11 Eliz. I, c. 9, *The Statutes at Large Passed in the Irish Parliaments Held in Ireland, 1310–1800* (20 vols, Dublin, 1786–1801), I, pp 322–38, and it was then copied by Campion in his *Historie of Ireland*, pp 141–2; for a discussion of its development and uses see Ciaran Brady, 'The killing of Shane O'Neill: Some new evidence', in *Irish Sword* XV (1982–3), pp 116–23, and 'The attainder of Shane O'Neill, Sir Henry Sidney and the problems of Tudor state-building in Ireland', in Ciaran Brady and Jane Ohlmeyer (eds), *British Interventions in Early Modern Ireland* (Cambridge, 2005), pp 28–48.

5 For a further development of this point concentrating largely on sympathetic fictional representations of Shane see Margaret Rose Jaster, 'Mythologising Shane O'Neill', in *New Hibernia Review / Iris Éireannach Nua* XI:3 (Autumn, 2007), pp 81–97.

6   John Mitchel, *The Life and Times of Aodh O'Neill, with Some Account of His Predecessors* (Dublin, 1845), ch. 2; Thomas O'Gorman, 'Notes on the career of Shane O'Neill (Seán an Díomais or 'the Proud')', in *Journal of the Royal Historical and Archaeological Society of Ireland*, 2nd series, VIII (1888), pp 449–62 and IX (1889), pp 53–8; 'Ollamh', *The Story of Shane O'Neill* (Dublin, n.d. [1903?]); Conan Máol (pseud.), *Seághan an Díomais: Blúirín ar Stair na hÉireann* [*Shane the Proud: A Fragment of Irish History*] (Dublin, 1901).

7   On this specific point, O'Gorman, 'Notes on the career of Shane O'Neill' is an exception.

8   For the contemporary belief that Catherine had colluded in the seizure of her husband and herself from the monastery in which they were being entertained, see Lord Justice Fitzwilliam to the earl of Sussex, 30 May 1561, TNA, SP 63/3/85.

9   *The Story of Shane O'Neill*, p. 32; P. J. Merriman, 'Shane O'Neill: A vindication', in *Journal of the Ivernian Society* (1912–13), pp 133–52 and 230–7.

10 Mitchel, *Life and Times of Aodh O'Neill*, p. 42.

11 For a brief discussion of this linguistic development see T. B. Lyons, 'Shane O'Neill: A Biography' (MA thesis, University College, Cork, 1948), pp ix–xi; see also John O'Donovan's notes in his edition of *Annála Ríoghachta Éireann: Annals of the Kingdom of Ireland by the Four Masters* (7 vols, Dublin, 1851), *s.aa* 1548, 1552 and 1565–7.

12 Ciaran Brady, 'The myth of Silken Thomas', in Peter Crooks and Sean Duffy (eds), *The Geraldines and Medieval Ireland: The Making of a Myth* (Dublin, 2016), forthcoming; also Laurence McCorristine, *The Revolt of Silken Thomas* (Dublin, 1987), pp 13–16.

13 Merriman, 'Shane O'Neill', p. 237: 'he made all his neighbours his enemies and this caused his fall. Not English power, but Irish rivalry brought the pride of Shane to the dust'; Moore, 'Shane O'Neill', p. 129: 'Shane's mistake was not to make a close union with the strongest of the other clans . . . his failure followed as the inevitable consequence.'

14 Brady, 'The attainder of Shane O'Neill'.

15 Ibid., pp 43–5.

16 On the standing of Geoffrey of Monmouth among the leading scholars of Tudor England see, T. D. Kendrick, *British Antiquity* (London, 1950), ch. 3; but on his contemporary uses see in particular Andrew Hadfield, 'Briton and

Scythian: Tudor representations of Irish origins', in *Irish Historical Studies* (Nov. 1993), pp 390–408.

17 'Act for the attainder of Shane O'Neill', esp. pp 324–8.

18 William Camden, *Annales Rerum Gestarum Angliae et Hiberniae Regnate Elizabetha* (London, 1615), *s.a.* 1562.

19 Lord Burghley's 'Memorandum', 20 Apr. 1574, TNA, SP 63/45/77; a modern edition of Sidney's 'Memoir of service' is supplied in Ciaran Brady (ed.), *A Viceroy's Vindication?: Sir Henry Sidney's Memoir of Service in Ireland* (Cork, 2002); one such inspired genealogy is to be found in TNA, SP 63/56/63 which, though it is part of an official report on the state of Ireland in 1576 during the viceroyalty of Sir Henry Sidney (author of the act of attainder), has sometimes surprisingly been accepted uncritically as an accurate statement of Shane's position; a slightly later, but equally inspired, English document, TNA, SP 63/65/6 enclosure II, (6 Jan. 1579) recognises two elder brothers of Shane as having been legitimate; but given the lateness, provenance and the immediate purposes behind such documents their correspondence to fact must be open to question.

20 'Humble petition of Hugh O'Neill, earl of Tyrone to Queen Elizabeth' ([Mar. 1587?]), TNA, SP 63/128/116.

Chapter 2: *The Problems of O'Neill Lordship, 1241–1541*

1 K. W. Nicholls, *Gaelic and Gaelicised Ireland in the Later Middle Ages* (2nd edn, Dublin, 2002) is an excellent general survey see esp. pp 151–66; for more detailed studies see Katharine Simms, 'Tír Eoghain "north of the mountain"', in Gerard O'Brien (ed.), *Derry and Londonderry: History and Society* (Dublin, 1999), pp 149–74 and 'Late medieval Tír Eoghain: The kingdom of the Great O Néill', in Charles Dillon, Henry Jeffries and William Nolan (eds), *Tyrone: History and Society* (Dublin, 2000), pp 127–62. See also Séamus Ó Ceallaigh, *Gleanings from Ulster History* (Cork, 1951); Thomas Matthews, *The O'Neills of Ulster: Their History and Genealogy* (3 vols, Dublin, 1907).

2 Simms, 'Tír Eoghain "north of the mountain"'; see also the map prepared by D. B. Quinn in Art Cosgrove (ed.), *A New History of Ireland: Volume II, Medieval Ireland, 1169–1534* (Oxford, 1987), p. 620.

3 On the origins of the O'Neills see James Hogan, 'The Irish law of kingship with special reference to Aileach and Cenel Eoghain', in *Proceedings of the Royal Irish Academy* XL (1931–2), sect. C, pp 186–254; Simms, 'Tír Eoghain "north of the mountain"' and 'Late medieval Tír Eoghain', but the most thorough account of O'Neill history in the later middle ages on which the

[3 *cont.*] articles just cited have been based, remains unpublished, M. K. Simms, 'Gaelic Ulster in the Late Middle Ages' (PhD thesis, University of Dublin, 1976), pp 622–788.

4   Simms, 'Gaelic Ulster', pp 672, 680–1,689–90,707–8 and 713–14; E. M. Jope, H. M. Jope and E. A. Johnson, 'Harry Avery's castle', in *Ulster Journal of Archaeology*, 3rd series, XIII (1950), pp 81–92.

5   Simms, 'Gaelic Ulster', pp 706–50; *Annála Ríoghachta Éireann: Annals of the Kingdom of Ireland by the Four Masters* (7 vols, Dublin, 1851) (hereafter *AFM*), *s.a.* 1432.

6   Simms, 'Gaelic Ulster', pp 756–68 and 778–82; *AFM*, *s.aa* 1479–81 and 1483 (for Énrí's resignation).

7   For an introductory survey of the O'Donnell's history in the later middle ages see Nicholls, *Gaelic and Gaelicised Ireland*, pp 162–4; for a more detailed accounts see Katharine Simms, 'Late medieval Donegal', Darren Mac Eiteagain, 'The Renaissance and the late medieval lordship of Tír Conaill, 1461–1555' and R. J. Hunter, 'The end of the O'Donnell lordship', all in William Nolan, Liam Ronayne and Mairead Dunleavy (eds), *Donegal: History and Society* (Dublin, 1995), pp 183–266.

8   Simms, 'Gaelic Ulster', pp 525–7 and 'Late medieval Donegal', pp 190–5.

9   Simms, 'Gaelic Ulster', ch. 8; Tom Murphy 'Creating facts on the ground: The destruction of Clandeboye', in *History Ireland* XX:3 (2012), pp 22–5.

10   Simms, 'Gaelic Ulster', pp 257–80.

11   G. A. Hayes-McCoy, *Scots Mercenary Forces in Ireland* (London, 1937), pp 15–76; for an account of the Scottish context see John Bannerman, 'The lordship of the Isles', in J. M. Brown (ed.), *Scottish Society in the Fifteenth Century* (London, 1977), pp 209–40; see also Andrew McKerral, 'West highland mercenaries in Ireland', in *Scottish Historical Review* XXX (1951), pp 1–14.

12   See in general George Hill, *An Historical Account of the MacDonnells of Antrim* (Belfast, 1873).

13   Two modern editions and translations of the *Ceart Uí Néill* are available: Myles Dillon (ed.), in *Studia Celtica* I (1966), pp 1–18, is highly scholarly; but the text and translation printed by Éamon Ó Doibhlin in *Seanchas Ardmhacha* V (1969–70), pp 324–58, comes supplied with a useful introduction and detailed commentary.

14   D. B. Quinn '"Irish" Ireland and "English" Ireland', in Cosgrove (ed.), *A New History of Ireland*, pp 621–3; Simms, 'Gaelic Ulster', pp 616–21.

15   Hill, *An Historical Account of the MacDonnells of Antrim*, ch. 2.

16   Brendan Smith, *Crisis and Survival in Late Medieval Ireland: The English of Louth and Their Neighbours, 1330–1450* (Oxford, 2013).

17 T. E. McNeill, *Anglo-Norman Ulster: The History and Archaeology of an Irish Barony, 1177–1400* (Edinburgh, 1980); the entry under 'Ulster' in G. E. C[okayne], *The Complete Peerage of England, Scotland, Ireland, Great Britain, and the United Kingdom Extant, Extinct, or Dormant* (2nd edn, 13 vols in 14 pts, London, 1910–59), XII, pt (II), pp 166–181, contains a wealth of pertinent information.

18 McNeill, *Anglo-Norman Ulster*, pp 21–36 and 98–128; see also Robin Frame, *English Lordship in Ireland, 1318–1361* (Oxford, 1982), pp 13–15 and 132–51 and 148–52.

19 G. H. Orpen, 'The earldom of Ulster', in *Journal of the Royal Society of Antiquaries of Ireland* XLIII (1913), pp 30–46 and 133–43; XLIV (1914), pp 51–66; XLV (1915), pp 123–42.

20 Katharine Simms, '"The King's friend": O'Neill, the crown and the earldom of Ulster', in James Lydon (ed.), *England and Ireland in the Later Middle Ages* (Dublin, 1981), pp 214–36.

21 Dorothy Johnston, 'The interim years: Richard II and Ireland', in Lydon (ed.), *England and Ireland*, pp 175–95, esp. pp 179–81; Simms 'The King's friend', pp 214–19.

22 Simms, 'The King's friend', pp 224–33.

23 Art Cosgrove, 'Anglo-Ireland and the Yorkist cause', in Cosgrove (ed.), *A New History of Ireland*, pp 557–68; D. B. Quinn, 'Aristocratic autonomy', in ibid., pp 591–610.

24 Simms, 'Gaelic Ulster', pp 781–8; Donough Bryan, *Gerald Fitzgerald, the Great Earl of Kildare, 1456–1513* (Dublin, 1933), *passim*.

25 *Stat. Ire., 12–22 Edw. IV*, quoted in Simms, 'Gaelic Ulster', p. 781.

26 Simms, 'Gaelic Ulster', pp 782–6; *AFM, s.aa* 1487–8 and 1498, and O'Donovan's notes to the entries.

27 For a succinct account see Mary Ann Lyons, *Gearóid Óg Fitzgerald* (Dundalk, 1998).

28 *State Papers during the Reign of Henry VIII* (11 vols, 1830–52), II, pp 40–1, 97–8 and 99–101 (hereafter *S. P. Hen. VIII*); *AFM, s.aa* 1522 and 1525–6; W. M. Hennessy (ed.), *Annals of Loch Cé* (2 vols, London, 1871), II, *s.a.* 1522.

29 *S. P. Hen. VIII*, II, pp 203–5, 226–31 and 247–9; on Conn Bacach's submission see Skeffington to O'Neill, ibid., pp 262–3.

30 Grey to Cromwell, 24 June 1536, ibid., II, pp 334–7.

31 Ciaran Brady, *The Chief Governors: The Rise and Fall of Reform Government in Tudor Ireland, 1536–88* (Cambridge, 1994), pp 13–25; Brendan Bradshaw, *The Irish Constitutional Revolution of the Sixteenth Century* (Cambridge, 1979), pp 174–85.

32 Grey to Cromwell, 31 Oct. 1538, J. S. Brewer and William Bullen (eds), *Calendar of Carew Manuscripts preserved in the Archiepiscopal Library at Lambeth,* 1515–74 (hereafter *Cal. Carew MSS, 1515–74*), pp 148–9.

33 Robert Cowley to Cromwell, 8 Sept. 1539, *S. P. Hen. VIII*, III, pp 145–9; *AFM, s.a.* 1539.

34 Bartholomew Warner to Sir John Wallop, 22 May 1540, *S. P. Hen. VIII*, III, pp 211–13; Brady, *Chief Governors*, pp 23–5.

35 St Leger and Council to Henry VIII, 28–29 Aug., 17 Dec. 1541, *S. P. Hen. VIII*, III, pp 313–20 and 350–3.

36 Ibid., pp 353–5; and for St Leger's support for the terms see ibid., pp 355–8.

37 Bradshaw, *Irish Constitutional Revolution*, pp 189–257.

38 St Leger and Council to Privy Council, 1 Sept. 1542, *S. P. Hen. VIII*, III, pp 416–18; *Cal. Carew MSS, 1515–74*, pp 188–93.

39 Henry VIII to St Leger, 14 Apr. 1542, *S. P. Hen. VIII*, III, pp 366–71.

40 James Morrin (ed.), *Calendar of Patent and Close Rolls of the Chancery in Ireland, Henry VIII to Elizabeth*, p. 85; *Cal. Carew MSS, 1515–74*, pp 198–9.

Chapter 3: *The Resistible Rise of Shane O'Neill, c. 1530–56*

1 *Annála Ríoghachta Éireann: Annals of the Kingdom of Ireland by the Four Masters* (7 vols, Dublin, 1851) (hereafter *AFM*); W. M. Hennessy (ed.), *Annals of Loch Cé* (2 vols, London, 1871), II, *s.a.* 1530 (hereafter *ALC*).

2 *AFM, s.a.* 1531, and O'Donovan's note to that year.

3 On fosterage practices see K. W. Nicholls, *Gaelic and Gaelicised Ireland in the Later Middle Ages* (2nd edn, Dublin, 2002), p. 79; see also the comments by J. A. Watt in Art Cosgrove (ed.), *A New History of Ireland: Volume II, Medieval Ireland, 1169–1534* (Oxford, 1987), p. 320.

4 Identification of Shane's place within the immediate family of Conn Bacach has been obscured by the process of posthumous mythologisation discussed in ch. 1 above; no Gaelic genealogies contemporary with his life have survived; the pedigrees on which assumptions have been based are to be found in TNA, SP 63/56/63 and SP 63/65/6 enclosure II.

5 Shane O'Neill's 'Answers' to articles submitted to him, 7 Feb. 1562, TNA, SP 63/5/22–3, and his later responses in J. S. Brewer and William Bullen (eds), *Calendar of Carew Manuscripts preserved in the Archiepiscopal Library at Lambeth,* 1515–74 (hereafter *Cal. Carew MSS, 1515–74*), pp 305–6.

6 On Feardorcha's activities see *AFM, s.aa* 1532 and 1540, and *State Papers during the Reign of Henry VIII* (11 vols, London, 1830–52), III, p. 358 (hereafter *S. P. Hen. VIII*). In 1542 he was, according to Campion, 'a lusty horseman . . .

and a tried soldier', Edmund Campion, *Two Bokes of the Historie of Ireland*, A. F. Vossen (ed.), (Assen, 1963), p. 138.

7   On Felim see W. M. Hennessy and B. MacCarthy (eds), *Annála Ulaidh: Annals of Ulster* (4 vols, Dublin, 1887–1901), IV, *s.a.* 1538; *AFM, s.a.* 1542; references to the other sons can be found in *S. P. Hen. VIII*, III, pp 355–8 and *Cal. Carew MSS, 1515–74*, pp 188, 191–3 and 234–5.

8   *S. P. Hen. VIII*, II, pp 355–8; Campion, *Two Bookes of the Historie of Ireland*, p. 138. Campion also described Shane at the time as 'little esteemed and of no proof', p. 134.

9   Thomas Phetyplace's report on Shane O'Neill, 16 May 1567, TNA, SP 63/20/92; O'Donovan's note in *AFM, s.a.* 1567.

10 See John O'Donovan's extensive note in *AFM, s.a.* 1567.

11 *AFM, s.a.* 1548.

12 'Article of complaint exhibited by the earl of Tyrone', 9 Feb. 1552, TNA, SP 61/4/7.

13 Sir Thomas Cusack to the earl of Warwick, 27 Sept. 1551, TNA, SP 61/3/52.

14 Ibid.

15 Nicholas Bagenal to Croft, 27 Oct., 11 Nov. 1551, TNA, SP 61/3/56, 65 enclosure I.

16 *Cal. Carew MSS, 1515–74*, p. 191.

17 Ibid., pp 188–91; for his royal pension see *Analecta Hibernica* I (1934), p.69.

18 Sir Thomas Cusack *et al.* to Privy Council, 22 Dec. 1552, TNA, SP 61/4/69.

19 Shane O'Neill to Queen Elizabeth, 8 Feb. 1561, TNA, SP 63/3/14.

20 Arbitration between O'Neill and O'Donnell, July 1543, Aug. 1545, July 1549, *Cal. Carew MSS, 1515–74*, pp 203–7, 214 and 220–2; Tyrone to Henry VIII, 1 May 1544, TNA, SP 60/11/4; Calvagh O'Donnel to Bellingham, 4 Jan. 1549, TNA, SP 61/2/2; *AFM, s.a.* 1548.

21 Arbitration of dispute between Tyrone, Maguire *et al.*, 20 June 1549, *Cal. Carew MSS, 1515–74*, pp 215–20; see also *S. P. Hen. VIII*, III, p. 571.

22 *ALC, s.a.* 1540; *S. P. Hen. VIII*, III, pp 354–6 and 434–6. In 1543 he is acknowledged as 'captain of his nation', *Cal. Carew MSS, 1515–74*, p. 208; his sudden but unexpected death is reported in *AFM* and *ALC, s.a.* 1544.

23 Bagenal to Croft, 27 Oct. 1551, TNA, SP 61/3/56.

24 See in general Tomás Ó Fiaich, 'The O'Neills of the Fews', in *Seanchas Ardmhacha* VII (1973), pp 1–64.

25 *S. P. Hen. VIII*, III, pp 353–6, 381–7 and 571; *Cal. Carew MSS, 1515–74*, pp 215–20.

26 St Leger and Council to Henry VIII, 6 May, 12 Aug. 1545, *S. P. Hen. VIII*, III, pp 517–20 and 524–33; Calvagh O'Donnell to Bellingham, 4 Jan. 1549; Privy

[26 *cont.*] Council to Bellingham, 6 Jan. 1549; Sir Thomas Cusack to Warwick, 27 Sept. 1551, TNA, SP 61/2/2, 3; 61/3/52.

27 George Hill, *An Historical Account of the MacDonnells of Antrim* (Belfast, 1873), ch. 3.

28 Ciaran Brady, *The Chief Governors: The Rise and Fall of Reform Government in Tudor Ireland, 1536–88* (Cambridge, 1994), pp 45–71; William Palmer, *The Problem of Ireland in Tudor Foreign Policy* (Woodbridge, 1994), chs 3–4.

29 On Bagenal in general see Brady, *Chief Governors*, pp 257–60; P. H. Bagenal, 'Sir Nicholas Bagenal, Knight Marshal', in *Journal of the Royal Society of Antiquaries of Ireland* XLV (1915), pp 5–26.

30 Brereton's 'Articles exhibited', Nov. 1550; St Leger to Somerset, 18 Feb. 1551; Irish Council to Privy Council, 20 May 1551, TNA, SP 61/2/66; 61/3/9, 25.

31 Brereton's 'Articles against Tyrone', Nov. 1550; St Leger to Cecil, 19 Jan. 1551; Irish Council to Privy Council, 20 May 1551; 'Complaints of the earl of Tyrone', 9 Feb. 1552, TNA, SP 61/2/76; 61/3/3, 25; 61/4/7.

32 See, for example, O'Neill to Henry VIII, Dec. 1541, 1 May 1544; Irish chieftains to Henry VIII, 23 Mar. 1546, TNA, SP 60/10/47; 60/11/41; 60/12/40; D. G. White, 'Henry VIII's Irish kerne in Scotland and France', in *Irish Sword* III (1957–8), pp 213–25.

33 St Leger to Cecil, 19 Jan. 1551; St Leger to Somerset, 18 Feb. 1551; St Leger to Privy Council, 23 Mar., 20 May 1551, TNA, SP 61/3/3, 9, 18, 25; see also Tyrone to St Leger, 9 Feb. 1552, and 'Report of conversation between St Leger and Tyrone', Mar. 1552, TNA, SP 61/4/9, 36.

34 Cusack to Warwick, 27 Sept. 1551; Bagenal to Croft, 27 Oct. 1551; Tyrone to Privy Council, 10 Apr. 1552; Cusack's 'Report' to Northumberland, 8 May 1552, TNA, SP 61/3/52, 56; 61/4/34, 43.

35 Cusack to Warwick, 27 Sept. 1551, 8 May 1552; Edward VI to Croft, Nov. 1551, TNA, SP 61/3/52; 61/4/43; 61/3/73; *AFM, s.a.* 1551.

36 Cusack's 'Report', 8 May 1552, TNA, SP 61/4/43.

37 Edward VI to Croft Nov. 1551, TNA, SP 61/3/73.

38 Cusack to Warwick, 27 Sept. 1551, TNA, SP 61/3/52.

39 Bagenal to Croft, 27 Oct., 11 Nov. 1551; Cusack's 'Report', 8 May 1552; Cusack *et al.* to Privy Council, 22 Dec. 1552, TNA, SP 61/3/56, 63 enclosure I; 61/4/43, 69.

40 Cusack to Warwick, 27 Sept. 1551; Cusack's 'Report', 8 May 1552; Cusack *et al.* to Privy Council, 22 Dec. 1552, TNA, SP 61/3/52; 61/4/43, 69.

41 *AFM, s.a.* 1552; Edward VI to Croft, 6 Nov. 1552, TNA, SP 61/4/62.

42 Cusack *et al.* to Privy Council, 22 Dec. 1552; 'Submission of Hugh MacNeill Oge', Edward VI to Tyrone, May 1553, TNA, SP 61/4/69, 73, 80.

43 Although he did not receive the job until November 1553, St Leger was actively advising the Privy Council on Irish affairs for almost a year previously.

44 'Letters to be written to the earls of Ireland', 1553; St Leger's 'Instructions', Oct. 1553, TNA, SP 61/4/85; 62/1/12.

45 *AFM, s.a.* 1554; for Shane's own account of events at this time see TNA, SP 63/5/23.

46 *AFM, s.a.* 1554; see also the later allegations made against Shane by the earl of Sussex, TNA, SP 63/5/31.

Chapter 4: *The Lost Peace, 1556–62*

1 *Annála Ríoghachta Éireann: Annals of the Kingdom of Ireland by the Four Masters* (7 vols, Dublin, 1851) (hereafter *AFM*), *s.aa* 1554–5; Sussex's 'Confutation', 14 Feb. 1562, TNA, SP 63/5/31.

2 *AFM, s.aa* 1558–9; for Shane's acceptance of responsibility for Dungannon's murder see his 'Answers', 7 Feb. 1562; see also Conn O'Neill to Queen Mary, June 1558, TNA, SP 63/5/23; 62/2/56.

3 On the significance of the ceremony see G. A. Hayes-McCoy, 'The making of an O'Neill: A view of the ceremony at Tullaghoge', in *Ulster Journal of Archaeology*, 3rd series, XXX (1970), pp 89–94.

4 *AFM, s.aa* 1556–7.

5 Ibid., *s.a.* 1555.

6 'Proclamation against Shane O'Neill', 8 June 1561, details Sussex's construction of Shane's actions since 1556; Shane's 'Answer' supplies a different interpretation of the same events, TNA, SP 63/4/13 enclosure 1; 63/5/23.

7 Sussex's 'Notes' for Elizabeth, Feb. 1559, TNA, SP 63/1/13.

8 *AFM, s.a.* 1557; Shane's 'Answer' and Sussex's 'Confutation', TNA, SP 63/5/23, 31.

9 Elizabeth's 'Instructions' to Sussex, 16 July 1559, J. S. Brewer and William Bullen (eds), *Calendar of Carew Manuscripts preserved in the Archiepiscopal Library at Lambeth*, 1515–74 (hereafter *Cal. Carew MSS, 1515–74*), pp 287–8.

10 Shane O'Neill to Elizabeth, *c.* Dec. 1559; Sussex's 'Memorial', May 1560; Elizabeth to Sussex, 15 Aug. 1560, TNA, SP 63/1/79; 63/2/21, 30.

11 For a general account of the war effort see Richard Bagwell, *Ireland under the Tudors* (3 vols, London, 1885–90), II, chs 19–20.

12 For a detailed account of the political developments, and preliminary negotiations leading up to the visit, see James Hogan, 'Shane O'Neill comes to the court of Elizabeth', in Seamus Pender (ed.), *Féilscríbhínn Tórna* (Cork, 1947), pp 154–70.

13 Sussex and the Irish Council to Elizabeth, 22 Nov. 1561, TNA, SP 63/4/72.

14 The details offered here are intended to qualify the historian William Camden's late and highly prejudiced account; compare Camden's *Annales Regnante Elizabetha, s.a.* 1562, with the brief contemporary references in J. G. Nichols (ed.), *Diary of Henry Machyn*, Camden Society 1st series, LXXIII (London, 1847), pp 274–7, and *Cal. S. P. Foreign, 1560–62*, p. 508.

15 O'Neills' submission, 6 Jan. 1562, *Cal. Carew MSS, 1515–74*, pp 311–12; but see the fuller account in TNA, SP 63/5/6.

16 The central elements of Shane's case are contained in the documents prepared for the debate of 7 Feb. 1562, TNA, SP 63/5/21–3.

17 The elements of Sussex's response are contained in TNA, SP 63/5/30–2.

18 Shane's 'Answers', 'Complaint' and 'Supplication', Mar. 1562, TNA, SP 63/5/22, 42, 45; *Cal. Carew MSS, 1515–74*, pp 305–8.

19 'Articles and covenants to be made with O'Neill', 20 Mar. 1562; Cecil's 'Memorandum', Mar. 1562, TNA, SP 63/5/43, 47–8.

20 See in particular Sir Henry Sidney's amendments, 11 Apr. 1562, TNA, SP 63/5/79; on Shane's willingness to compromise on the introduction of English legal structures see his 'Answer', 25 Mar. 1562, TNA, SP 63/5/63.

21 Elizabeth to Lord Justice Fitzwilliam, 13 Mar. 1562, O'Neill to Elizabeth in reply [13 Mar.] and Cecil's memorandum [*c.* 13 Mar.], TNA, SP 63/5/42–4.

22 Ciaran Brady, 'Shane O'Neill departs from the court of Elizabeth: Irish, English and Scottish perspectives and the paralysis of policy, July 1559 to Apr. 1562', in S. J. Connolly (ed.), *Kingdoms United? Great Britain and Ireland since 1500: Integration and Diversity* (Dublin, 1999), pp 13–28; on the primacy of Anglo-Scottish relations in Cecil's thinking at this time see Stephen Alford, *The Early Elizabethan Polity: William Cecil and the British Succession Crisis* (Cambridge, 1998).

23 Cecil's 'Memorandum', Mar. 1562, and Elizabeth to Lord Justice Fitzwilliam, 13 Mar. 1562, TNA, SP 63/5/43–4.

24 Fitzwilliam to Elizabeth, Cecil and the Privy Council, 14 Apr. 1562; Shane to Privy Council, 2 Apr. 1562; Articles of Covenant, 30 Apr. 1562; Shane to Elizabeth, 2 May 1562; Elizabeth's 'Proclamation' in favour of Shane, 5 May 1562, TNA, SP 63/5/61, 82–4, 99; 63/6/6/2, 6.

25 On Sussex's attitude toward Ireland and the character of his administration in general see Ciaran Brady, *The Chief Governors: The Rise and Fall of
Reform Government in Tudor Ireland, 1536–88* (Cambridge, 1994), ch. 3.

26 See Sussex's 'Opinion touching the Reformation of Ireland', Sept. 1560,
Cal. Carew MSS, 1515–74, pp 300–4.

27 *AFM, s.a.* 1554; Hogan, 'Shane O'Neil comes to the court of Elizabeth'.

28 Sussex's 'Opinion', Sept. 1560, Dec. 1562, *Cal. Carew MSS, 1515–74*, pp 300–4
and 330–44.

29 Sussex to Cecil, 19 Aug. 1561, TNA, SP 63/4/37.

30 The older view on the importance of faction as represented by J. E. Neale,
'The Elizabethan political scene', in his *Essays in Elizabethan History* (London,
1958), pp 59–84, and Wallace MacCaffrey, 'Place and patronage in Elizabethan
politics', in S. T. Bindoff *et al.* (eds), *Elizabethan Government and Society:
Essays* presented to Sir John Neale (London, 1961), pp 95–126 has been
challenged by Simon Adams, 'Faction, clientage and party: English politics,
1550–1603', in *History Today* XXXII (1982), pp 33–9, and 'Eliza enthroned? The
court and its politics', in Christopher Haig (ed.), *The Reign of Elizabeth*
(London, 1984), pp 55–77 and most radically in Alford, *The Early Elizabethan
Polity*, ch. 2.

31 Alford, *The Early Elizabethan Polity*, ch. 3.

32 On the complex circumstances surrounding the return of Mary Stuart to
Scotland and the responses of the Scottish nobility to the prospect see in
general J. E. A. Dawson, 'Two kingdoms or three? Ireland in Anglo-Scottish
relations in the middle of the sixteenth century', in Roger A. Mason (ed.),
Scotland and England, 1286–1815 (Edinburgh, 1987), pp 113–38.

33 'Articles agreed upon at Berwick', 27 Feb. 1560, *Cal. S. P. Foreign, 1559–60*,
p. 414.

34 Shane to Argyll, and Argyll to Elizabeth, July 1560; Cecil to Argyll, 2 Apr.
1561; Sussex's 'Instructions' to William Hutchinson', 27 Apr. 1561, TNA, SP
63/2/26; 63/3/49, 60.

35 Sussex's 'Memorial', May 1560, Elizabeth to Sussex, 15 Aug. 1560, Sussex's
'Instructions' to William Hutchinson, 27 Apr. 1561, TNA, SP 63/2/26, 30; 3/60.

36 Fitzwilliam to Sussex and to Cecil, 30 May 1561, TNA, SP 63/3/ 84, 85.

37 Dawson, 'Two kingdoms or three?', pp 122–4; *Cal. S. P. Scotland, 1547–63*,
pp 593 and 603–4.

38 Jones review of Alford, 'Early Elizabethan polity', in *Albion: A Quarterly
Journal Concerned with British Studies* XXXI:3 (Autumn, 1999), pp. 467–9.

39 Brady, *Chief Governors*, pp 91–3 and 102–3.

40 Conyers Read, *Mr Secretary Cecil and Queen Elizabeth* (London, 1955), ch. 10; Wallace MacCaffrey, *The Shaping of the Elizabethan Regime* (London, 1968), chs 5–6.

41 Alford, *Early Elizabethan Polity*, chs 2–3.

Chapter 5: *Appeasement and Drift, 1562–5*

1 Anonymous letter to Shane, *c.* Mar./Apr. 1562; Fitzwilliam to Cecil, 29 Apr., 28 May, 19 June 1562; Shane to Elizabeth, 2 Nov. 1562, TNA, SP 63/5/62, 98; 63/6/14, 26; 63/7/39.

2 Sussex to Cecil, 1 Aug., 21 Sept. 1562; Sussex to Elizabeth 27 Aug., 29 Sept., 5 Oct. 1562, TNA, SP 63/6/62 75; 63/7, 11, 19, 29.

3 Sussex to Cecil, 21 Sept., 4 Dec. 1562; Sussex to Privy Council, 26 Oct., 28 Dec. 1562, TNA, SP 63/7, 16, 34, 53, 58.

4 Wallace MacCaffrey, *The Shaping of the Elizabethan Regime* (London, 1968), ch. 6 and *Elizabeth I* (London, 1993), ch. 7.

5 Shane to Elizabeth, Dudley and Cecil, 2 Nov. 1562, TNA, SP 63/7/39–41.

6 Ciaran Brady, *The Chief Governors: The Rise and Fall of Reform Government in Tudor Ireland, 1536–88* (Cambridge, 1994), pp 102–7.

7 Sussex to Privy Council, 20 May 1563, TNA, SP 63/8/47.

8 Sussex and Council to Privy Council, 26 May 1563, TNA, SP 63/8/50.

9 Sussex to Elizabeth, 29 Sept. 1562; Elizabeth to Sussex, 15 Oct. 1562, TNA, SP 63/7/19; 9/32. Described in official correspondence as 'my lord treasurer's man' and 'the queen's footman', Smyth was in secret negotiations with Shane at the time, TNA, SP 63/7/19, 32,41, 10/38; for an earlier attempt to assassinate Shane, see Sussex to Elizabeth, 24 Aug. 1561, TNA, SP 63/4/42.

10 Sussex to Elizabeth, 29 Sept. 1563, Elizabeth to Sussex, 15 Oct. 1563, TNA, SP 63/7/19; 63/9/32.

11 Cusack's 'Memorial', 6 Aug. 1563, TNA, SP 63/8/64.

12 Elizabeth to Sussex, 7 Aug. 1563, TNA, SP 63/8/47.

13 Brady, *Chief Governors*, pp 105–6.

14 'Form of a peace made between . . . the Queen's commissioners and Shane O'Neill', 11 Sept. 1563, TNA, SP 63/9/9, also in abbreviated calendared form in J. S. Brewer and William Bullen (eds), *Calendar of Carew Manuscripts preserved in the Archiepiscopal Library at Lambeth*, 1515–74 (hereafter *Cal. Carew MSS, 1515–74*), pp 352–4.

15 Quotation from article 1 of the 'peace'.

16 For the treaty and related subsequent negotiations see TNA, SP 63/9/9 and *Cal. Carew MSS, 1515–74*, pp 352–4; see also 'Articles of indenture' and Shane's 'Petitions', 18 Nov. 1563, TNA, SP 63/9/60, 62–5; also Shane O'Neill to Lord Robert Dudley, 29 Feb. 1564, *Report on the Pepys Mss at Magdalene College, Cambridge* (Historical Manuscripts Commission, 1911), p 63.

17 Cusack to Cecil, 22 Mar., 17 Apr. 1564; Privy Council to Cusack, 2 Apr. 1564, TNA, SP 63/10/38, 42, 51.

18 Cusack to Cecil, 22 Mar. 1564; Privy Council to Cusack, 2 Apr. 1564, TNA, SP 63/10/38, 42.

19 Brady, *Chief Governors*, pp 107–9.

20 Cusack to Dudley, 9 June 1564; Shane to Arnold, 18 Aug., 5 Sept. 1564; Arnold to Shane, 22 Aug. 1564, TNA, SP 63/11/3, 76, 80.

21 Shane to Arnold, 5 Sept. 1564; Dean Donnelly to Arnold, 5 Sept. 1564, TNA, SP 63/11/83, 84.

22 Cusack to Privy Council and to Dudley, 8–9 June 1564; Calvagh O'Donnell's 'Requests' and 'Answers', 12 June 1564; Wrothe to Cecil, 18 June 1564; Conn O'Donnell to Cusack, 20 Nov. 1564; Elizabeth to Arnold, 3 Dec. 1564, TNA, SP 63/11/1, 3, 10–12, 103, 110.

23 Elizabeth to Arnold, 3 Dec. 1564, TNA, SP 63/11/110.

24 Arnold's 'Note on the state of Ireland', 29 Jan. 1565, TNA, SP 63/12/20.

25 For detailed accounts see George Hill, *An Historical Account of the MacDonnells of Antrim* (Belfast, 1873), pp 132–9 and J. Michael Hill, 'Shane O'Neill's campaign against the MacDonnells of Antrim, 1564–5', in *Irish Sword* XVIII:71 (Summer 1991), pp 129–38.

26 Shane to Arnold, 2, 22 May, 18 June 1565; Gerard Fleming to Cusack, June 1565; Privy Council to Shane, 22 June 1565, TNA, SP 63/13/34, 48, 66, 71, 82.

27 J. E. A. Dawson, 'Two kingdoms or three? Ireland in Anglo-Scottish relations in the middle of the sixteenth century', in Roger A. Mason (ed.), *Scotland and England, 1286–1815* (Edinburgh, 1987), pp 125–9.

28 Brady, *Chief Governors*, pp 111–12 and 119–21.

Chapter 6: *War, 1566–7*

1 Elizabeth's 'Instructions' concerning Shane, 12 Nov. 1565, TNA, SP 63/15/42.

2 On Knollys see in general the sketch in *Oxford Dictionary of National Biography* [*ODNB*] s.v.; Knollys to Cecil, 19 May 1566; Cecil's 'Notes', 30 May 1566, TNA, SP 63/17/20, 56, 70.

3   Elizabeth to Sidney, 8 July 1566, TNA, SP 63/18/46; on arrangements in September see TNA, SP 63/19/3–6.

4   J. E. A. Dawson, 'Two kingdoms or three? Ireland in Anglo-Scottish relations in the middle of the sixteenth century', in Roger A. Mason (ed.), *Scotland and England, 1286–1815* (Edinburgh, 1987); *Cal. S. P. Scotland, 1563–8*, pp 223, 240, 254, 277 and 282–94.

5   Shane to Charles IX and the Cardinal of Lorraine, 25 Apr. 1566, TNA, SP 63/17/34–5.

6   Sidney gives a detailed account in his 'Memoir of service', in Ciaran Brady (ed.), *A Viceroy's Vindication? Sir Henry Sidney's Memoir of Service in Ireland* (Cork, 2002), pp 44–7; but see his contemporary reports of 12 Nov. 1566, TNA, SP 63/19/43, 44.

7   Sidney to Cecil, 20 Nov. 1566; Edward Horsey to Cecil, 21 Nov. 1566; Thomas Lancaster to Cecil, 23 Nov. 1566; Privy Council to Sidney, 12 May 1567, TNA, SP 63/19/52–3, 57; 63/20/84.

8   Sidney, 'Memoir of service', pp 48–9.

9   Sidney and Council to Elizabeth, 22 Nov. 1566; Shane to John of Desmond, 9 Sept. 1566; Shane to Sidney and Council, 29 Dec. 1566, TNA, SP 63/19/7, 55; 63/20/13 enclosure I.

10   Sidney to Elizabeth, 20 Apr. 1567, TNA, SP 63/20/67.

11   For a full and brilliant account see 'Farsetmore, 1567', in G. A. Hayes-McCoy, *Irish Battles* (London, 1967), pp 68–86, and also Tomás Ó Brógáin, 'The battle of the Swilly (Farsetmore) 8 May 1567', in *History Ireland* XIX (May/June 2011), pp 16–18.

12   *Annála Ríoghachta Éireann: Annals of the Kingdom of Ireland by the Four Masters* (7 vols, Dublin, 1851), *s.a.* 1567.

13   Ibid.; the annalists suggest, in a further indication of the early spread of the myth of 'Shane the Proud' that Shane had temporarily lost his reason. The story of the halter is first mentioned in the act attainting Shane (*Stat. Ire.*, I, 327–8) and should therefore be treated with skepticism for the reasons discussed in ch. 1.

14   Ciaran Brady, 'The killing of Shane O'Neill: Some new evidence', in *Irish Sword* XV (1982–3), pp 116–23.

15   Sidney's 'Memorial of things not expressed in the letters', [15] June 1567, Elizabeth to Sidney, 6 July 1567, TNA, SP 63/21/20, 49

16   This account is based on the earliest contemporary report, William Fitzwilliam to Sir William Fitzwilliam, July 1567, edited in Brady, 'The killing of Shane O'Neill'.

17 Edmund Campion, *Two Bokes of the Historie of Ireland*, A. F. Vossen (ed.), (Assen, 1963), pp 139–41; the significance of the event, but more importantly the role of Piers in managing its occasion, is evident in the fact that Piers was awarded the extraordinary sum of 1,000 marks (£666.66) from the Irish treasury in thanks for his service, TNA, SP 63/71/53.

Conclusion

1 A. J. P. Taylor, *The Origins of the Second World War* (Penguin edn, Harmondsworth, 1964), 'Second thoughts', p.27. Any association of Shane with Hitler is, of course, preposterous; it would be regrettable if any earlier gestures toward Taylor's inspiring and provocative study of inter-war diplomacy should be mistaken in such a manner.

2 In so far as it occurred, and the evidence, it should be noted, comes from an embattled Sidney as he prepared for a major campaign against O'Neill, this was an apparently late phenomenon, Sidney to Leicester, 1 Mar. 1566, and 'Answers' of Thomas Phetyplace, 16 May 1567, TNA, SP 63/16/35, 20/92.

3 See pp 73–4 above.

4 On the structural dysfunctions of Elizabethan administrative and political system see Penry Williams, *The Tudor Regime* (Oxford, 1979) and A. G. R. Smith, *The Government of Elizabethan England* (London, 1977).

5 Classic statements of the view that the laws and institutions on the English constitution underpinned the polity's remarkable stability are *Sir John Fortescue, De Laudibus Legum Angliae* [1471], ed. S. B. Chrimes, (Cambridge, 1942), and Sir Thomas Smith, *De Republica Anglorum* [composed 1562–5], ed. Mary Dewar, (Cambridge, 1982).

6 See pp 6–9 above.

7 Ciaran Brady, *The Chief Governors: The Rise and Fall of Reform Government in Tudor Ireland, 1536–88* (Cambridge, 1994), ch. 4 above.

Select Bibliography

Shane O'Neill has fallen into disrepute. In the late nineteenth and early twentieth centuries he was the subject of a large number of monograph-length essays which either denounced him or attempted, often with great difficulty, to place him within the Irish nationalist tradition (see notes to chapter 1 above). But this body of writing revealed throughout a persistent tendency to accept as given personal characteristics, most especially his pride and his violence, which were derived almost exclusively from hostile sources either contemporary or later.

The remarkable tendency to reinforce the myth of Shane the Proud is explored most entertainingly in Margaret Rose Jaster, 'Mythologising Shane O'Neill', in *New Hibernia Review / Iris Éireannach Nua* XI:3 (Autumn, 2007), pp 81–97. One of the most curious findings of Jaster's essay is that, as scholarly interest in Shane languished, he became the central figure of several novels, notably E. B. Barrett, *The Great O'Neill* (Boston, 1939), Elizabeth Linington (aka Dell Shannon), *The Proud Man* (New York, 1955), and most recently P. L. Henry, *Ulster is Mine* (Galway, 2002).

In this context it is perhaps significant that the most extended scholarly study of Shane remained unpublished: T. B. Lyons's excellent MA thesis, 'Shane O'Neill: A Biography' (University College, Cork, 1948). In the historiography of the later twentieth century, Shane has featured in several new interpretative works which have provided a different context within which his career may be assessed, but none have essayed any substantial revision of his status; see Ciaran Brady, *The Chief Governors: The Rise and Fall of Reform Government in Tudor Ireland, 1536–88* (Cambridge, 1994); Nicholas Canny, *The Elizabethan Conquest of Ireland: A Pattern Established, 1565–76* (Hassocks, 1976); and Colm Lennon, *Sixteenth Century Ireland: The Incomplete Conquest* (Dublin, 1993). Two contrasting surveys of events in Ulster in the later sixteenth century are Hiram Morgan, 'The end of Gaelic Ulster: A thematic interpretation of events between 1534 and 1610', in *Irish Historical Studies* XXVI (1988), pp 8–32, and Ciaran Brady, 'Sixteenth century Ulster and the failure of Tudor reform', in Ciaran Brady, Mary O'Dowd and Brian Walker (eds), *Ulster: An Illustrated History* (London, 1989), pp 77–103. See also the opening section of Hiram Morgan, *Tyrone's Rebellion: The Outbreak of the Nine Years War in Tudor Ireland* (Woodbridge, 1993) and also of Darren McGettigan, *Red Hugh O'Donnell and the Nine Years War* (Dublin, 2005).

Since James Hogan's promising essay 'Shane O'Neill comes to the court of Elizabeth', in Seamus Pender (ed.), *Feilscribhínn Tórna* (Cork, 1947), pp 154–70, there have been few detailed studies dealing directly with Shane himself, and among those the circumstances of his death have, oddly enough, assumed most prominence: see Ciaran Brady, 'Shane O'Neill departs from the court of Elizabeth: Irish, English and Scottish perspectives and the paralysis of policy, July 1559 to April 1562', in S. J. Connolly (ed.), *Kingdoms United? Great Britain and Ireland since 1500: Integration and Diversity* (Dublin, 1999), pp 13–28; 'The killing of Shane O'Neill: Some new evidence', in *Irish Sword* XV (1983), pp 116–23; 'The attainder of Shane O'Neill, Sir Henry Sidney and the problems of Tudor state-building in Ireland', in Ciaran Brady and Jane Ohlmeyer (eds), *British Interventions in Early Modern Ireland* (Cambridge, 2005), pp 28–48; Prionsias Ó Conluain, 'Shane O'Neill's postbag: His letters from Benburb and the woods', in *Duiche Neill* I (1988), pp 1–28; and Caoimhin Breathnach, 'The murder of Shane O'Neill: Oidheadh chuinn cheadchathaigh', in *Ériu* XLIII (1992), pp 159–76. J. Michael Hill, 'Shane O' Neill's campaign against the MacDonnells of Antrim', in *Irish Sword* XVIII (1991) is a valuable study in military history. The same author's *Fire & Sword: Sorley Boy MacDonnell and the Rise of Clan Ian Mór, 1538–90* (London, 1993) is, along with Morgan's and McGettigan's work cited above, one of the few deeply researched scholarly monographs concerned with any of the major figures of later sixteenth-century Ulster.

In recent years scholars of English and Scottish history have shown a greater awareness of the broader parameters of their political worlds in the later sixteenth century, recognising the importance of developments in Ireland, and particularly in Ulster in relation to other regions. Especially good examples of this development are Christopher Maginn, *William Cecil, Ireland, and the Tudor State* (Oxford, 2012), Stephen Alford, *The Early Elizabethan Polity: William Cecil and the British Succession Crisis* (Cambridge, 1998) and Jane E. A. Dawson, *The Politics of Religion in the Age of Mary, Queen of Scots: The Earl of Argyll and the Struggle for Britain and Ireland* (Cambridge, 2002). Wallace Mac Caffrey, *The Shaping of the Elizabethan Regime* (London, 1968) remains as an authoritative account of the complex and changing atmosphere of the early Elizabethan court.

But the most fruitful approach for a deeper understanding of O'Neill's age would seem to lie in the study of the individual Ulster lordships in the later Middle Ages and the sixteenth century. In this regard the series of county histories published by Geography Publications under the 'History and Society' subtitle has produced invaluable works. See among the most relevant volumes A. J. Hughes and William Nolan (eds), *Armagh: History and Society* (Dublin, 2001), Gerard O'Brien (ed.), *Derry and Londonderry: History and Society* (Dublin, 1999), William Nolan, Liam Ronayne and Mairéad Dunleavy (eds), *Donegal: History and Society* (Dublin, 1995), Eileen Murphy and William Roulston (eds), *Fermanagh: History and Society* (Dublin, 2004), and Charles Dillon, Henry Jeffries and William Nolan (eds), *Tyrone: History and Society* (Dublin, 2000). In addition to several of her seminal contributions to these volumes see also for general context and trends Katharine Simms's invaluable, *From Kings to Warlords* (Woodbridge, 1985); two older county histories by Peadar Livingstone are still useful, *The Fermanagh Story* (Enniskillen, 1969) and *The Monaghan Story* (Enniskillen, 1980). George Hill, *An Historical Account of the MacDonnells of Antrim* (Belfast, 1873) remains a classic.

Index